ARMS CONTROL AND SECURITY

For Sue and Stefan

Arms Control and Security

The changing role of conventional arms control in Europe

KEVIN WRIGHT
University of Essex

Ashgate

Aldershot • Burlington USA • Singapore • Sydney

Published by
Ashgate Publishing Limited
Gower House
Croft Road
Aldershot
Hampshire GU11 3HR
England

Ashgate Publishing Company
131 Main Street
Burlington
Vermont 05401
USA

Ashgate website: http://www.ashgate.com

British Library Cataloguing in Publication Data
Wright, Kevin
        Arms control and security : the changing role of
        conventional arms control in Europe
        1. Arms control - Europe 2. National security - Europe
        I. Title
        327.1'74'094

Library of Congress Control Number: 00-132796

ISBN 1 84014 470 X

Printed in Great Britain by
Antony Rowe Ltd, Chippenham, Wiltshire

Contents

List of Tables

About the Author

Kevin Wright, is a Teaching Fellow in the Department of Government at the University of Essex. He teaches primarily in the field of international relations and on the European Union. He works and writes extensively on conventional arms control issues, the European security architecture and the emerging security threats facing the North Atlantic area.

Preface

The conclusion of the Conventional Armed Forces in Europe Treaty in 1990, the series of Vienna Documents from 1990 onwards and the Treaty on Open Skies in 1992 were agreements, along with those applying to nuclear weapons, which were intended to enable Europe to look forward to a future overshadowed less by military affairs than had been possible for the previous fifty years.

The reality however has been far from this expectation. Wars of succession have taken place in the former Yugoslavia and on the territory of the former Soviet Union, whilst ethnic tensions have grown in other parts of Central and Eastern Europe too. At the same time the old alliance structure has collapsed with the dissolution of the Warsaw Treaty Organisation and a NATO scrambling to reinvent itself in a radically different security environment. NATO forces have been actively engaged militarily in the Balkans in a role very different from that envisaged during the Cold War for Alliance forces.

In all of this melee arms control and confidence building has taken on an increasingly lower priority, indeed the approach taken during the Cold War, often look increasingly outdated, if not entirely obsolete. Yet at the same time the continuing military contacts required and fostered by the major arms control agreements of the 1990s still has a value.

The aim of this book is to explore the changing role of conventional arms control in Europe. The early chapters provide a primarily historical perspective looking at the context, foundations, main provisions and institutional structure of the main agreements. The later chapters explore the continuing and likely future roles of the OSCE and NATO in the arms control process. The final chapters examine more contemporary developments by looking at the Adapted CFE Treaty and Vienna Documents agreed at the OSCE Istanbul Summit in November 1998 and the challenges posed to existing arrangements by the changing and emergent security threats that potentially face Europe.

Throughout the book in undertaking the examination of this important area of security policy I have adopted an epistemic community/network approach. As is explained in chapter 1 this methodology, though it is incomplete and has weaknesses, provides a useful way of understanding the advances and developments made in the mid-nineteen eighties and why progress has become more difficult since.

In putting together this work of necessity I have received a great deal of assistance from officials within NATO, the OSCE Secretariat, the United Kingdom Ministry of Defence and the UK Delegation to the OSCE in Vienna. My thanks to all of those concerned. Most important of all however are 2 further people: Professor Emil Kirchner and Lynda Hudson both at the University of Essex. Professor Kirchner for getting me started on this project in the first place and providing much advice and assistance well beyond the call of duty. My thanks to Lynda are for her preparedness to read the many drafts of chapters and correcting the large number of my mistakes, normally at times when she had much better things to do.

Any mistakes or omissions are, of course, entirely my own responsibility.

Kevin Wright
University of Essex

List of Abbreviations

ACDA	Arms Control & Disarmament Agency (US)
ACDU	Arms Control & Disarmament Research Unit (FCO)
ACFE	Adapted CFE Treaty
ACV	Armoured Combat Vehicle
ACVC	Arms Control Verification Centre
AIAM	Annual Implementation Assessment Meeting
AIFV	Armoured Infantry Fighting Vehicle
APC	Armoured Personnel Carrier
ATTU	Atlantic to the Urals
BWC	Biological Weapons Convention
CBM	Confidence Building Measure
CDE	Conference on Disarmament in Europe
CEE	Central & Eastern Europe
CFE	Conventional Forces in Europe
CFE 1A	Concluding Act of the Negotiation on Personnel Strength of Conventional Armed Forces in Europe
CFSP	Common Foreign & Security Policy (EU)
CiO	Chairman in Office (OSCE)
CIS	Commonwealth of Independent States
CPC	Conflict Prevention Centre
CSBM	Confidence Security Building Measures
CSCE	Conference on Security Co-operation in Europe
CSO	Committee of Senior Officials (OSCE)
CWC	Chemical Weapons Convention
DTRA	Defence Threat Reduction Agency
EAPC	Euro-Atlantic Partnership Council
EU	European Union
FCO	Foreign & Commonwealth Office
FSC	Forum for Security Co-operation
FSU	Former Soviet Union

GEMI	Global Exchange of Military Information
GRIT	Graduated and Reciprocated Initiatives in Tension reduction
HLTF	High Level Task Force
HLWG	High Level Working Group
IAEA	International Atomic Energy Authority
IFOR	Implementation Force (NATO)
INF	Intermediate Nuclear Forces Treaty
IW	Information Warfare
JACIG	Joint Arms Control Implementation Group
JCC	Joint Consultative Commission
JCG	Joint Control Group
KFOR	Kosovo Force
KVM	Kosovo Verification Mission
MBFR	Mutual and Balanced Force Reduction
MBT	Main Battle Tank
MFA	Ministry of Foreign Affairs
MoD	Ministry of Defence
MTCR	Missile Technology Control Regime
MURFAAMCE	Mutual Reductions of Forces and Armaments and Associated Measures in Central Europe -also known as MBFR
NAC	North Atlantic Council
NACC	North Atlantic Co-operation Council
NATO	North Atlantic Treaty Organisation
NNA	Neutral and Non-Aligned
NPT	Non-Proliferation Treaty
NSSM	Norm-and Standard Setting Measure
NSWTO	Non-Soviet Warsaw Treaty Organisation
NTM	National Technical Means
OOV	Objects of Verification
OSCC	Open Skies Consultative Commission
OSCE	Organisation for Security and Co-operation in Europe
OSI	On-Site Inspection
OSIA	On-Site Inspection Agency
PACS	Proliferation & Arms Control Secretariat (UK MoD)

PfP	Partnership for Peace
PIA	Programme for Immediate Action
POE	Point of Entry
POET	Protocol on Existing Types
POM	Passive Overflight Module
REACT	Rapid Expert Assistance and Co-operation Teams
SAR	Synthetic Aperture Radar
SDC	Special Disarmament Commission
SDR	Strategic Defence Review
SFOR	Stabilisation Force (NATO)
SRCC	Sub-Regional Consultative Commission
TLE	Treaty Limited Equipment
TNS	Telephone Notification System
UFV	Unite Francaise de Verification
VCC	Verification Coordination Committee
VD	Vienna Documents
VERITY	NATO Arms control information database
VERTIC	Verification Technology Information Centre
VICS	Verification Implementation Cooperation Section (NATO)
VU	Verification Unit
WEU	Western European Union
WGA	Working Group A (FSC)
WGB	Working Group B (FSC)
WMD	Weapons of Mass Destruction
WTO	Warsaw Treaty Organisation
ZvBW	Zentrum fur Verification der Bundeswehr

1 European Conventional Arms Control: Importance, Conceptions and Definitions

This chapter establishes the background for the rest of the book by examining some of the basic elements of arms control. It is undertaken by briefly outlining that in an uncertain Europe, the Western part of the continent appears extremely stable whilst Central, Eastern and Southern Europe is experiencing greater instability than it has for at least the last fifty years. In such a situation arms control and confidence building potentially still have a substantial part to play in reducing those instabilities. This is followed by a quick examination of some of the distinctions between arms control and confidence building and the political and technical functions of verification. This has a continued practical significance because of the agreement structure currently in place as it casts a shadow into the future shaping, to some extent, what developments might take place in the future. This leads onto a section which outlines the contemporary context in which further policy is being made and implemented. The 'theoretical lens' which this book utilises are the ideas of 'epistemic communities' and 'policy-networks' which gained currency during the mid-nineteen nineties in other areas of international relations. The main tenets of these theoretical concepts are explored, their relationship to conventional arms control in Europe is outlined which is then pursued in greater detail through individual chapters in the rest of the book.

This approach appears to some advantages for a better understanding of this policy area as it attempts to capture the element of 'high' politics of diplomatic negotiation and how this is translated into practical effect by officials and military personnel. It allows account to be taken of technical expertise in the field in the negotiation and implementation which is balanced against part played by concepts of 'national interest' in the policy process. A 'meso' level approach it offers opportunity to examine how outcomes in terms of practical experiences derived from policy operation can be fed back into the policy process where technical expertise and understanding is often at a premium.

Europe after the Cold War

The 'earthquake' events in Europe since 1989 which saw the fall of the Berlin Wall, the collapse of communist regimes in Central and Eastern Europe and the eventual demise of the Soviet Union have resulted in a massive reappraisal of where Europe stands and in what direction it should look to the future. Looking at those possibilities has become a major industry and concern for academics, journalists, civil servants, military officers and politicians to name just some. The views of the future they predict are almost as diverse as the people producing them with the assessments ranging from highly optimistic to extremely pessimistic. Many questions revolve upon the effects change might have on 'stability', balances of power, international organizations and the nature and extent of cooperation in the international system.

The result has been a proliferation of literature and a resurgence of interest in security issues speculating and predicting a whole range of possible outcomes. There are also efforts to widen the definition of security beyond its traditional military emphasis with which we have lived during the Cold War.[1] Much of this literature deals with possible roles for international organizations, the prospects for cooperation in the realms of security and economics and predictions of the 'security architecture' that might finally emerge for Europe.

At one extreme, pessimistic views of change, such as those from John Mearsheimer, predict the increased probability of major conflict and crises within Europe resulting from the fracturing of bi-polarity, based upon assumptions that it is the 'distribution and character of military power that are the root causes of war and peace'.[2] Kenneth Waltz follows not dissimilar lines of arguments, suggesting that NATO will disappear and what will eventually emerge is a complicated balance of power, until, or unless, superpowers develop which rival the USA.[3] Others, including Kegley and Raymond, reflect that the assertion 'that multi-polarity produces instability' is a somewhat premature conclusion.[4] Concentration on the options for major state actors - particularly the United States and Russia have been major preoccupations.

The Cold War emphasis was very much on the problems of military security. However, since 1989 there has been a marked tendency to try and downplay the role of military issues. In its place notions of economic, societal and environmental security have come to the fore spawning a wide tide of literature extolling the roles that each will play in future. Ole Wœver, Barry Buzan et al have introduced models of 'societal security' and how they are important in securing peace in Europe.[5] Buzan describes these changes and argues that some of the new challenges that will emerge as being profound. These all suggest that military aspects of security will be relegated to the background.[6] However, the avoidance of war and the mitigation of its effects alone are powerful motives for suggesting that confidence building and arms control still have a role to play.

Whatever the theoretical predictions and speculations about the future, events themselves have not been entirely encouraging. NATO is still adjusting to the disappearance of the Warsaw Pact, old conflicts have remerged in former communist states, war has destroyed former Yugoslavia and strife has, and continues to affect, a clutch of former Soviet republics. The use of military force, and equally as important, its potential application as a tool of conflict resolution has far from disappeared. Indeed there has been a marked tendency to resort to military violence as we have seen in the former Soviet Republics and the Balkans. On the territory of the old Yugoslavia NATO has 'gone to war' for the first time since its creation and at a time when some had come to regard it as a redundant organisation.

Are we witnessing the tidying up of 'loose-ends' left by the finish of the Cold War, or are a set of more fundamental fissures beginning to emerge? Is Kalevi Holsti correct in his assertion that a major problem of peace settlements of the past is that they have always attempted to deal with the causes of previous crises rather than identifying newly emerging ones? If he is, the existing confidence building and arms control system could already be obsolescent. Conversely they could still be significant tools for managing part of Europe's military security relationships for sometime to come.[7] In a climate of uncertainty measures that warn, restrain, constrain and defuse military means of conflict resolution in Europe are important. These mechanisms in the forms of confidence and security building measures (CSBM's) and arms control agreements, which have a significant role in reducing military uncertainty were rapidly agreed in the early 1990s. Measures that promote trust and confidence in the conduct of military relations, by providing an appreciation of capabilities and operations are of importance, not only in their own right, but have a wider significance if they can also contribute to stability and reduce the likelihood of military conflict. Success in this area ought to permit significant reductions in military expenditure, through lower troop and equipment levels and reduce the burdens military expenditure imposes - especially important to overstretched Central and East European transition economies.

The CSBM agreements in Europe have generally been politically, but not legally, binding and this aspect of their design, with its lack of necessity for lengthy ratification procedures is often cited as a major reason for their success.[8] Whilst virtually all the major European states as well as the United States and Canada have entered into these agreements, few are prepared to accept other states - especially those of former adversaries - adherence to the terms of the agreements purely on trust. Virtually all participants regard it as necessary to verify or confirm compliance with agreements in some form. Yet in both financial and resource terms verification has proved an expensive business whilst the benefits are not always clearly discernable.

Distinctions between Arms Control and Confidence-Building

While it is at least technically and theoretically feasible to draw a distinction between the roles of arms control and CSBM's, they are usually considered to be interlinked, frequently interdependent concepts. CSBM's are generally considered to be just one element of arms control. Further, it is difficult to contemplate a situation where arms control could advance significantly without at least some confidence between its participants that all parties will abide by the agreement. Similarly it is difficult to envisage situations where increased confidence cannot, at the very least, open further opportunities that could lead to the willingness to engage in further arms control measures. This potential for a 'snowball effect' in promoting further trust and co-operation is often cited as an attribute of arms control and confidence building measures.

To illustrate the degree of overlap between the concepts Holsti outlines five categories of arms control measures.[9] He talks of *architectural measures*, designed around the political fabric of European states and *structural measures* covering the size and composition of military forces. Holsti's third category of *operational measures* relates to peacetime constraints on the operations of military forces, whilst *exchange measures* concern force structure and force planning details. The final grouping is of *declaratory measures* that describe state and bloc intentions. Here it is the third and fourth categories of this classification that are described by others as being the defining elements of CSBMs.

Mackintosh and Slack discuss two definitions of CSBM's, one based upon broad functional principles of confidence building which can accommodate all styles of CSBM's without being restricted to single narrow examples.[10] The second model attempts to isolate what confidence building actually *does* and *why*. The essence of confidence-building here revolves around the concept that the process aims to develop and enhance *basic confidence*[11] to be evidenced in that 'all states participating in the negotiations essentially have non-hostile intentions'.[12] Nevertheless a functional model of confidence building is a much more difficult one to satisfactorily define in a form which permits close empirical study.

Volker Rittberger et al have defined a number of characteristics that CSBMs possess.[13] These include the exchange of information, forms of state behaviour that help to eliminate the causes of tension, and promoting habits of co-operation between potential adversaries. They should also be capable of helping to restore equilibrium during periods of international tension, and include techniques for verification to protect against deception. The key distinction from the measures that Rittberger draws is that CSBM's deal with the *operations* of military forces not their *capabilities*. Even from such a brief comparison of the two concepts undertaken here it is possible to see that there is a wide degree of potential for overlap between the two.

It is Rittberger's key distinction, with its emphasis on operations, that is utilized throughout this study. As he makes clear to use wide definitions of arms control, which include CSBMs as an integral element of it, removes their status as distinct diplomatic tools that can be used to promote security co-operation whilst at the same time avoiding possibly contentious issues of force structure and numbers of weapons.[14] This very much reflects the reality of the situation for inter-bloc negotiations in Vienna during the 1980s. The uneasiness of this relationship was perpetuated through the separation of the 'stability' and 'reduction' talks which were held at the same time in the Hofburg Palace, but in different parts of the building to maintain some formal facade of separation.

Cuthbertson and Robertson make a comparable point by stating that security is not just a function of manpower strengths and equipment levels but what rivals *do* with their manpower and weapons.[15] The significance of this point must not be lost. Whilst there are a number of important domestic and international factors that influence European states to adopt particular military postures, the existence and operation of a comprehensive and reliable CSBM regime, has the potential to reduce mutual fears of neighbouring states and the possibilities for unintentional arms races and 'accidental' conflict.[16]

The Dimensions of Verification

The Functions of Verification

The inadequate development of satisfactory verification measures was often cited as the cause for the stumbling of negotiations during the Cold War, although on occasions it was also the excuse for the lack of progress too.[17] In very few instances has participants compliance been judged solely upon trust. In modern international arms control and confidence building agreements verification measures are seen as *the* means of ensuring compliance, but are also perceived as having additional positive 'side effects' in terms of aiding 'transparency'.

Defining the functions of verification is a complex undertaking because the focus of interest for scholars and policy actors is often not the end product of the verification, in stark terms of confirming compliance or violation, but more often what is facilitated as a result of this evaluation which is in turn dependant on actors motivations. A preliminary list of the functions attributed to verification at various times include: checking compliance, preventing cheating, increasing transparency, increasing confidence, furthering cooperation, facilitating organizational change/development, punishing violation, rewarding compliance and minimizing exploitation. Therefore verification is not just a technical process it is one that is essentially 'political' too.

Verification as a Technical Issue

The actual task of verifying compliance, as a technical issue, utilizing the broad definition of it comprising 'the human, technological and procedural resources' establishes wide parameters. Initially discussion can be separated into quantitative (numerical) and qualitative (capabilities and intentions) elements for problem solving but it should also be appreciated that for the operational military the two concepts frequently have a strong inter-relationship.

To try and observe these quantitative and qualitative elements at the operational military level a number of techniques can be utilized. All require the use of a combination of human, technical and procedural resources. These are the use of:

- On Site Inspections.
- The use of stand off or remote sensors.

•   International data exchange.

1.On Site Inspections. On Site Inspections (OSIs) are traditionally viewed as one of the most rigorous and intrusive methods of ensuring compliance with agreements and their use was at the heart of debate between East and West on verification arrangements for many years. However such inspections can become incredibly complicated and expensive as it has with the CFE Treaty.

OSI's can be used in the qualitative sense that they are opportunities for closely examining at first hand items of equipment and comparing them with established baselines or exchanged data. In the qualitative sense close examination of equipment can help to establish its potential uses. Similarly observation of exercises and manoeuvres can be an indicator of military doctrine and operational capabilities.

However, OSI's as well as being procedurally complicated and costly can also face difficulties in actually classifying and counting items of externally similar equipment when certain items are agreement limited and others are not.[18] As well the use of OSI's in military operational circumstances they are also a viable method to monitor production.[19]

2. The use of Stand Off Sensors. Stand off sensors -often airborne systems such as satellites, reconnaissance aircraft, ground installations or naval vessels whether equipped with optical, thermal, radar or electronic sensors - have been the acceptable face of espionage during the Cold War.

During the Cold War such sensors operating from friendly or international territory, waters or airspace were continually used by the Soviet Union and United States in particular to gather information on the other's activities. Usually operated on a purely national basis such sensors can equally be used in many circumstances as part of the verification process. The quantitative role that these sensors can fulfil can be limited by their technical sensitivity e.g. whilst, say, a radar picture might be able to determine that a vehicle is present it might not be able to differentiate between a truck or a tank.

In a qualitative sense, backed by high quality data assessment, and a knowledge of different military doctrines the information provided by these sensors can add considerably to the stock of knowledge on capabilities and intentions. However, as useful as such data can be for the quantitative assessment the qualitative element should be regarded more suspiciously. Such evaluation is much more sensitive to the quality of the assessment made by its evaluators. As valuable as high quality assessment can be poor interpretation, or worse mis-interpretation can be disastrous in times of tension or crisis.

3. International Data Exchange.   International data exchange is considered a key element of the arms control and CSBM agreements that have been reached in Europe to date. In fact reliable data exchanges could theoretically form the entire basis for such agreements, if there was no fear of accidental misunderstanding or deliberate manipulation. Data exchange is not only a valid method for the passing of quantitative information based on either established baseline or ongoing changes, which is considerably cheaper than the other two options, but it can have considerable qualitative possibilities too.

Whilst these three methods might provide the opportunities for observing and/or measuring possession, operation, deployment their value is strictly limited without sound qualitative assessment capabilities to support the observation. This vital, complementary adjunct to the technical element of verification is thus a 'political' element, although this too requires some clarification.

Verification as a Political Issue

From the discussion above it can be said that observation and evaluation are intricately linked concepts. Whilst the former may involve technical and, by implication almost 'scientific' legitimacy the latter is almost entirely a political construct. Verification has a number of stages. It begins with monitoring using some or all of the methods of data collection outlined above. However, the next stage, compliance evaluation, is a much more a political construct as there is no 'impartial jury' available to adjudicate compliance but it is the agreements parties that must resolve any difficulties between themselves.[20] If differences cannot be resolved then there is a range of responses available up to, and including, treaty withdrawal that can be considered.

What are the 'political' elements of verification? Essentially they revolve around 'policy' - policy making and its implementation. In the 1960s and 1970s conventional arms control was largely stalemated. Policy, such as it was, was largely restricted to the national level, and even intra-alliance policy coordination was extremely limited. It was only during the 1980s that conventional arms control became a more dynamic policy area. The internal determination of state positions, coordination with allies, agreement with other participants, administrative implementation arrangements, evaluation and dispute resolution mechanisms all became more 'real' and important as agreements were negotiated and achieved. All of these are integral to policy making and development subject to political judgement, determination and decision.

The Policy Relevance of Arms Control Verification

Mention of verification as both a technical and a political issue illustrates some of the complexities involved. This discussion also shows that verification is a difficult issue to address in isolation. First, the early stages of serious negotiations on conventional arms control from the MBFR talks onwards, but more particularly the late 1980s, required the development of appropriate negotiating positions and supporting policy to fill an empty 'policy space'. Reaching these agreements brought obligations, whilst the necessity for their verification involved the engagement of expertise at political and technical levels.

The forms of technical expertise required of conventional arms control negotiations and verification are diverse. They require understanding military staff structures, formation and unit organisation, military doctrine, force deployment and disposition, functions of equipment and its main characteristics and capabilities from the smallest unit to entire national force structures. These are of course extremely wide areas of expertise, representing specialisms in their own right. When turning to verification technologies, there are optical, infra red, radar, photographic and others too. All have their particular applications that makes them useful in different sets of circumstances. They often require a technical-scientific appreciation to understand their particular advantages and disadvantages to given situations.

Thus negotiators are faced with having to take technical scientific advice to inform or guide internal policy choices to review competing ideas or proposals. Of course negotiators are not only influenced by technical scientific factors but also more strategic and political choices too. As examples how would NATO allies react to one of its members states accepting a low ceiling on the number of tanks it can possess, if a state regards naval or air power as more important to its strategic choices than investment in land forces? If a state is just in the process of purchasing large numbers of attack helicopters, is it prepared to accept the domestic criticism it might face in cancelling the order, because of its effect on employment or does it just lobby for a higher proportion of attack helicopters to be allocated to it? What will be the financial and resource costs of collecting and interpreting all the data from verification provisions and what gains will it give? Thus such considerations, and many others, have to be factored into domestic policy choices before they even reach the international level at NATO or in Vienna.

Inadequacies of Structural Approaches

The search for answers in structural terms suggests a state centred approach to the problem and also implies that the actors are largely rational ones. Such models also have to take account of the distribution of power within Europe. This is easier and more plausible in the period prior to 1989 where the USA and USSR could be perceived almost as 'gatekeepers' controlling what came into and out of the process but by no means monopolizing what went on in between.[21] After 1991 the process becomes more difficult to identify in this vein as the Soviet Union disintegrated and the US adopted a lower profile involvement in Europe. Such an abstracted level of explanation lacks important detail which could, if it were added, make the explanation more convincing. However, if greater detail is added to the model then the approach begins to lose some of its initial credibility as resort is made to more complex explanations and generalities in order to maintain the consistency of the approach.

Another structural model employed concentrates on the differential power levels that existed between the USA and Soviet Union as being a key factor in regime formation.[22] When the power differential is high then the model asserts that the level of co-operation is low but as the differential decreases the potential for regime formation is increased. Applying the model one can find at least superficial relationship to account for the lack of development of security co-operation between 1945 and the early 1980s and then why it picked up pace between 1985 to 1990. It could also account for a lack of progress since the collapse of the Soviet Union as the power differential between the USA and Russia, as the main Soviet successor state, rapidly increased again. Even though this differential has increased, Russia has still continued to participate in major security institutions, has not been exceptionally obstructive; all of which must cause some doubt to be cast validity of this model.

The problem with the sort of structural approach outlined above is that their outlook is so global, so over-arching, that whilst in general terms they provide intuitively plausible explanations for a number of situations, they are neither comprehensive nor convincing. Whilst using such a grand scale of explanation, applying it to a single specific, set of circumstances and/or events may appear to provide an adequate 'fit' the explanation remains unconvincing because the structural models tend to be insufficiently detailed to in-depth evaluation. This may help to account for the greater weight generally accorded to the use of sub-systemic variables of regime formation. Utilizing a sub-systemic variable approach, to analyse the existing CSBM and arms control system, means that the level of study becomes much more manageable.

health community know each other's ideas, proposals and research, and often know each other very well personally. As an unobtrusive indicator of these interactions, I asked respondents to name others to whom I should speak. The same names would rather quickly surface as I went from one person to the next, suggesting that the circle of specialists was fairly small and fairly intimate.[31]

Policy communities are attributed with some distinctive features that make them different from policy networks and stability has a particular importance. Thus Jordan describes a policy community as

> A special type of *stable* network, which has advantages in encouraging bargaining in policy resolution. In this language the policy network is a statement of shared interests in a policy problem: a policy community exists where there are effective shared 'community' views on the problem. *Where there are no such shared views no community exists.*[32]

It is also considered important that membership should be highly restrictive with a difficulty in accepting and absorbing new members. To support this contention Richardson cites some of Rhodes work saying

> policy communities are networks characterised by stability of relationships, continuity of highly restrictive membership, vertical independence based upon shared delivery responsibilities and insulation from other networks and invariably from the general public.[33]

This restrictive membership component is supported by other authors who suggest that there are 'rules of the game' which actors have to abide by if they want to become insiders to the community, where institutional exclusion can be used as a methodology to restrict membership by granting membership of the most central institutions to only 'approved' groups or individuals. Exclusion is also said to be by degrees where a policy community has a 'core' and a 'periphery'. At the core are those with unrestricted access and participation whilst towards the edge are those who do not have enough resources to exert a continuous influence on the policy process, whilst others still are completely excluded.[34] Another factor discussed is that policy communities are often the product of institutionalised structural power.[35]

However, in the literature on epistemic communities we can find a much more detailed definition of a model, deliberately designed for application at the level of international politics with state centric politics embedded in its approach. Thus with its detailed framework, the importance it ascribes to state action, whilst recognizing that international cooperation in a whole range of policy areas increasingly requires the involvement of technical expertise, makes the epistemic community approach one that offers a strong possibility for understanding and explaining the rapid developments of European conventional arms control since the mid 1980s.

Peter Haas and Epistemic Communities

Peter Haas argues that structural and power based arguments of international politics often overlook the possibility that states can actually learn new patterns of reasoning. This permits states to adopt new interests and to take advantage of the considerable latitude for action still available to them. The term 'epistemic communities' has its origins and general usage with reference to scientific communities but more recently usage has been broadened to include groups from many disciplines that share a number of common qualities.[36]

Haas suggests an epistemic community is one that is comprised of a:

> network of professionals with recognized expertise and competence in a particular domain and a substantive claim to policy relevant knowledge in that domain or issue-area.[37]

He also says that these communities can be comprised of individuals from a variety of disciplinary backgrounds and professions as long as they share a number of common factors which include:

- A shared set of normative and principled beliefs (these provide a value based rationale for the action of community members).

- Shared causal beliefs, which are derived from their analysis of a situation, contribute to understanding a central set of problems which then serves as the basis for establishing linkages between possible policy actions and desired outcomes.

- Shared notions of validity that are intersubjective and give communities internally defined criteria for validating knowledge in their areas of expertise.

• A common policy enterprise -a set of common practices associated with the problems they wish to see resolved coupled with the conviction that human existence will be enhanced as a result. [38]

The common policy enterprise is considered a central part of the formal definition of an epistemic community. However, Sebenius suggests that those enterprises need not always be explicitly framed ones but can also be implicit.[39]

Haas suggests that the role of these communities of knowledge based experts are considerable in the articulation of cause and effect relationships of complex problems, helping states identify their interests, framing issues for collective debate, proposing specific policies and the identification of salient points for negotiation. Haas argues that the control over knowledge and information is an important element of power, the diffusion of new ideas can lead to new patterns of state behaviour and prove an important determinant of policy coordination.[40]

Whilst the logical progression of the notion is relatively simple the dynamics of policy coordination is subject to uncertainty, interpretation and the extent of institutionalisation. In this context uncertainty in situations where there is a dependence on other states in order to determine their own policy actions to achieve success, or where the consequences of particular courses of action are not entirely estimable, or are likely to generate a demand for information. In such situations it is suggested that the information required is not one that 'best guesses' others actions or where there is 'raw data' to be assessed. What is required in situations where inter-related physical or social processes that need highly specialized, complex, technical or scientific interpretation of social and physical phenomenon are involved is evaluative resources which are available to participants either in a domestic or international context.[41] Peter Haas suggests epistemic communities are one such method of obtaining this information. He asserts that as the demand for information arises, so too do the communities that can service that need. These communities can become strong actors at national and international level as their views are sought by decision-makers.

The growth of transnational communities may well influence states interests or preferences both directly or indirectly by helping to identify salient points from which states can then deduce relevant issues and their own interests. As an epistemic community gains and develops its influence in different governments, national policies and preferences come to reflect those epistemic beliefs.[42] Key state decision makers may also influence other states decision makers in terms of interests or behaviour more directly. This combination may well result in more convergent state behaviour and international policy coordination. Similarly the existence of expert communities may well contribute to the creation and maintenance of social institutions that guide international behaviour. The end result might be the creation of forms of patterned behaviour in a given issue area that persist long after the original systemic power concentrations are no longer sufficient to compel states to coordinate their activities.[43]

Haas argues that the epistemic approach can be used to illustrate the diffuse manner in which new ideas are taken into account by decision makers and identifies that there can be non-systemic origins for state interest definition. It also illuminates a dynamic for persistent cooperation that is independent of the international distribution of power. Other researchers suggest that the epistemic communities arguments are supplementary ones whereby the emergence of 'new knowledge' allows the pursuit of entirely new objectives, but are still shaped by power distributions and capabilities.[44] One conclusion of the research is that whilst specific policy choices can be influenced by epistemic communities, this is heavily conditioned by systemic situations and the nature and distribution of power between states.[45] Hence it is reasonably easy to envisage situations where complex agreements can be reached in a given policy area which are then quickly disposed of in the process of package dealing across a range of issues. Jeremy Richardson reaches similar conclusions, through different reasoning by suggesting that the definitions of communities run the danger of overlooking the linkages in, and between, policy communities that mean, even with their involvement, policy outcomes often escape their grasp because they are agreed within much wider decision-making configurations.[46]

The Dimensions of a Putative Conventional Arms Control Epistemic Community

The small numbers of people in the specialized field of conventional arms control possess a knowledge base and competence that has a relevance for policy makers. Whilst the case for the existence of an epistemic community in conventional arms control remains to be proved it is possible to outline a number of locations for the existence of potential expertise in the area. A grouping of expertise has developed that is spread between:

- National OSCE Delegations in Vienna.
- NATO Headquarters in Brussels.
- National capitals.
- National verification agencies.

The greatest number of people involved are those within the verification agencies (on implementation), whilst those working within national defence ministries, foreign ministries and national delegations to Vienna and NATO represent a much smaller number and proportion. In terms of actual numbers, with the exception of the US and Russia, the numbers of officials substantially involved in conventional arms control policy work, probably number only 7-10 for the larger and medium sized states spread between capitals, Vienna and NATO (where appropriate). For the smaller states, particularly those of the newly independent states, often rely on 4 or less people. Both Russia and the United States each maintain a substantially larger presence - over 20 staff - though many of these are only present for periods of about 3 months.

From the locations identified above the state centric nature of the field is clearly visible. Individual state decision-making processes are to a greater or lesser extent (depending on the state concerned), pluralistic in that whilst national capitals might have the final say, they also rely on input from their delegations in Vienna and Brussels. In the case of the United States which has a 'multi-agency' approach, its policy is developed with input from the National Security Council, State Department, Arms Control and Disarmament Agency (ACDA), Defence Threat Reduction Agency, parts of Defence Department, Commerce Department, Energy Department, intelligence community, Congress and specialist non-governmental organisations to name just the major actors the situation is considerably more complex.[47] Williams and Rogers illustrate the strongly competitive domestic dimension to arms control policy-making that can exist saying:

> The vagaries of bureaucratic and domestic politics in Washington in particular, meant that internal negotiations were sometimes even more time consuming and complex and than the negotiations with the adversary.[48]

However, non-governmental influences on conventional arms control have been relatively small. The advice and information processes in the field of arms control are internally developed and utilized by defence and foreign affairs ministry bodies with little external input from specialist groups and the academic community.

The extent of these individual groupings, their place in the policy-making and implementation processes is explored more fully in the succeeding individual chapters. Within the specific locations it is also necessary to determine at what 'levels' any putative community might operate. Is it at the policy-making level? Or is it the 'operational' level of implementation? What is the nature of the relationship, if any, between the two? What part do politicians, officials and 'implementers' play in the overall policy process?

Conclusions

The conclusions to be drawn from such as introductory chapter as this are somewhat limited. We certainly have a Europe that is unsettled if not unstable in its entirety. The problems that have beset a dissolved Soviet Union and Yugoslavia are evidence of this alone. The certainty of bi-polarity is gone, even though what will replace it in the longer terms ids far from certain. From that it is relatively straightforward to deduce that arms control and confidence building still have a substantial role to play in the management of military relations across the continent. The definitions that have been examined covering the concepts of arms control and confidence building are still current, even if the context and level at which they operate are somewhat different to that which applied at the beginning of the 1990s. They also explain why it is preferable in historical, theoretical and practical terms to continue to make the distinctions between arms control and confidence building. The added element that did not really exist in any substantial form prior to the 1990s was verification. The practical experience of operating the agreements which were reached came to show very quickly that the political functions are at least as important as its technical function, and that the technical element is not nearly as clinical as it was believed it would be.

The section on epistemic communities and policy networks covers a number of elements. On the one hand we have a theoretical approach that attempts to find a place for expertise and organisational learning through a 'community' that is ascribed some very specific functions. On the other hand we have an 'empty' policy space (conventional arms control) where common understandings and a detailed technical vocabulary had to be quickly agreed (despite years of disagreement during the MBFR talks). This combination of empty policy space and the need for a specialised and technical knowledge appear to make it a strong candidate for the existence of an epistemic community. At the same time the existing theoretical approaches for explaining the advances in arms control are unconvincing because they lack important detail. Therefore examining the rapid development of European conventional arms control and confidence building from an epistemic perspective appears to offer strong possibilities for advancing understanding of both.

Notes

1   For a general review of 'Traditionalist' and 'Copenhagen School' concepts of security see: B. Buzan, (1997), 'Rethinking Security after the Cold War', *Cooperation and Conflict*, Vol. 32, No. 1, pp. 5-28.

2   J. Mearsheimer, (1990), 'Back to the Future: Instability in Europe After the Cold War', *International Security*, Vol. 15, No. 1, pp. 5-6.

3   K. Waltz, (1993), 'The New World Order', *Millennium: Journal of International Studies*, Vol. 22, No. 2, p. 194.

4   C. Kegley and G. Raymond, (1992), 'Must We Fear a Post-Cold War Multipolar System?', *Journal of Conflict Resolution*, Vol. 36, No. 3, p. 573.

5   See O. Wœver, (1993), 'Societal security: the concept' and B. Buzan, 'Societal security, state security and internationalization', in O. Wœver, B. Buzan, M. Kelstrup and P. Lemaitre, (eds), *Identity, Migration and the New Security Agenda in Europe*, (London: Pinter Publishers).

6   B. Buzan, (1993), Ibid. p. 2.

7   J. Holsti, (1991), *Peace and war: armed conflicts and international order 1648-1989*, (Cambridge: CUP), p. 344.

8   F. Schimmelfennig, (1993), *Arms Control and the Dissolution of the Soviet Union: Regime Robustness and International Socialization*, Tubinger Arbeitspapiere Zur Internationalen Politik Und Friedensforschung, Nr 21, p. 26.

9   J. Holsti, (1991), 'Arms Control in the Nineties', *Daedalus*, Vol. 120, No. 1, pp. 96-100.

10   J. Mackintosh and M. Slack, (1989), 'Confidence-building in the Arctic', in *Sovereignty and Security in the Arctic*, Dosman, E., (ed), (London: Routledge), pp. 127-28.

11   Emphasis added.

12   J. Mackintosh and M. Slack, (1989), op. cit. p. 129.

13   V. Rittberger, M. Efinger and M. Mendler, (1988), *Confidence and Security Building Measures (CSBM): An Evolving East-West Security Regime*, Tubinger Arbeitspapiere Zur Internationalen Politik Und Friedensforschung, (Tubingen: Tubingen University) Nr 8, pp. 12-13.

14   Ibid. p. 15.

15   I. Cuthbertson and D. Robertson, (1990), *Enhancing European Security: Living in a Less Nuclear World*, (Basingstoke: Macmillan), p. 186.

16   For a discussion of definitions of arms races and how they can begin and escalate, see C. Anderton, (1988), 'A survey of arms race models' in *Arms races, arms control and conflict analysis*, W. Isard, (ed), (Cambridge: Cambridge University Press), pp. 17-20.

17   N. Gallagher, (1994), *Reaching Agreement on Verification: The Role of Interests, Ideas and Internal Politics*, APSA Conference, November 1994, p. 8.

18   See for example discussions on the CFE case study and 'Coming in from the Cold', transcript of *Horizon*, BBC TV (1991), p. 6.

19   See for example the discussions by I. Oelrich, (1990), 'Monitoring production of conventional weapons' in S. Koulik, and R. Kokoski, (eds), *Verification of Conventional Arms Control in Europe*, (Oxford: Westview Press).

20   T. Findley, (1988), *Bear Skins and Skunk works: The Politics of Verification*, Working Paper 43 (Canberra: Peace Research Centre, Australian National University), p. 7.

21   V. Rittberger, M. Efinger and M. Mendler, (1988), *Confidence and Security Building Measures (CSBM): An Evolving East-West Security Regime*, Tubinger Arbeitspapiere Zur Internationalen Politik Und Friedensforschung, Nr 8., (Tubingen: Tubingen University), pp. 18-19.

22   M. Effinger & Rittberger, (1992), 'The CSBM Regime in and for Europe: Confidence Building and Peaceful Conflict Management', Pugh, M.C., (ed), *European Security - Toward 2000*, (Manchester: Manchester University Press), pp. 104-23.

23   G. Dudley and J. Richardson, (1996), 'Why does policy change over time? Adversarial policy communities, alternative policy arenas, and British trunk roads policy 1945-95', *Journal of European Public Policy*, Vol. 3, No. 1, pp. 63-83. H. Kassim, (1994), 'Policy Networks, Networks and European Union Policy Making: A Skeptical View', *West European Politics*, Vol. 17, No. 4, pp. 15-27. J. Peterson, (1995), 'Policy Networks and European Union Policy Making: A reply to Kassim', *West European Politics*, Vol. 18., No. 2, pp. 389-407. J. Peterson, (1995), 'Decision-Making in the European Union: towards a framework for analysis', *Journal of European Public Policy*, Vol. 2, No. 1, pp. 69-93. C.M. Radaelli, (1995), 'The role of knowledge in the policy process', *Journal of European Public Policy*, Vol.2, No. 2, pp. 159-83. J.J. Richardson, (ed), (1996), *European Union: Power and Policy-Making*, (London: Routledge). D. Josselin, (1996), 'Domestic policy networks and European negotiations: evidence from British and French financial services', *Journal of European Public Policy*, Vol. 3, No. 3, pp. 297-317.

24   H. Kassim, (1994), op. cit. p. 16.
25   R.A.W. Rhodes, (1992) in H. Kassim, op. cit. p. 17.
26   M.J. Smith, (1993), *Pressure, Power and Policy: State autonomy and policy networks in Britain and the United States*, (London: Harvester Wheatsheaf), p. 57.
27   J. Peterson, (1995), 'Policy Networks and European Union Policy Making: A reply to Kassim', *West European Politics*, Vol. 18, No. 2, p. 391.
28   Ibid. p. 391.
29   J.W. Kingdon, (1984), *Agendas, Alternatives, and Public Policies*, (Boston: Little Brown Books).
30   K. Wright, (1998), *European Conventional Arms Control and Epistemic Communities*, PhD thesis, (University of Essex).
31   J.W. Kingdon, (1984), op. cit. p. 123.
32   G. Jordan, (1990), in J.J. Richardson, (ed), (1996), *European Union: Power and Policy-Making*, (London: Routledge), p. 7.
33   D. Marsh and R.A.W. Rhodes, (eds), (1992), *Policy Networks in British Government*, (Oxford: Clarendon Press), p.13. and M.J. Smith, (1993), op. cit p. 62.
34   M.J. Smith, (1993), op. cit. p. 61.
35   Ibid. p. 73. and P. Haas, (1992), 'Introduction: epistemic communities and international policy co-ordination', *International Organisation*, Vol. 46, No. 1, p. 2.
36   P. Haas, (1992) op. cit. pp. 2-3.
37   Ibid. p. 3.
38   Ibid. p.3.
39   J. Sebenius, (1992), 'Challenging conventional explanations of international cooperation: negotiation analysis and the case of epistemic communities', *International Organisation*, Vol. 46, No. 1, pp. 352.
40   P. Haas, (1992), op. cit. p. 3.
41   Ibid. p. 4.
42   P. Haas, (1995), 'Epistemic Communities and the Dynamics of International Environmental Co-Operation', in V. Rittberger, (ed), *Regime Theory and International Relations*, (Clarendon Press, Oxford), p. 188.
43   P. Haas, (1992), op. cit. p. 4.
44   Ibid. p.4.
45   Ibid. p. 7.
46   J.J. Richardson, (1996), 'Policy-making in the EU', in J.J. Richardson, (ed), (1996), op. cit pp. 7-8.
47   A. Sands, (1998), 'The Impact of the Governmental Context on Negotiation and Implementation: Constraints and Opportunities for Change', in N.W. Gallagher (ed), *Arms Control: New Approaches to Theory and Policy*, (Frank Cass: London), pp. 117-118.

48   J. Rogers and P. Williams, (1994), 'The United States and CFE' in S. Croft, (ed), *The Conventional Armed Forces in Europe Treaty*, (Dartmouth: Aldershot), p. 69.

2 The 1980s: Rapid Progress and the Changing Political Environment

This chapter briefly tracks some of the major causes and events during the rapid period of the conventional arms control negotiations between East and West during the 1980s. It does so in a relatively straightforward manner, which inevitably omits some detail, but illustrates state pre-eminence in the negotiation process. It will be seen that discussions and negotiations were undertaken in the 'traditional' diplomatic manner. But changes in the Soviet leadership, followed by a reappraisal of policy objectives, required the Soviets to adopt a negotiating perspective that was previously only held by the West. Pursuing those new objectives, created a degree of convergence that contributed to the creation of a negotiating space. This new space allowed agreements to be reached in a rapidly changing and complex matrix of domestic and international relationships. This negotiation space permitted diplomats and technical experts, to emerge as a group familiar with the language, and sharing some broad mutual aims that enabled advances to become consolidated and developed further. To complement this towards the end of the chapter the relationship between the existence of a possible epistemic community in the field and the Vienna talks during the 1980s and early 1990s is explored.

Background

Between 1973 and 1989 the Mutual and Balanced Force Reduction talks (MBFR), or more accurately, the 'Negotiations on the Mutual Reductions of Forces and Armaments and Associated Measures in Central Europe (MURFAAMCE), was the only forum for the discussion of East-West conventional arms control issues.' Involving as 'direct participants' both superpowers, the UK and Canada, they also included affected states in the area defined as 'Central Europe' -the GDR, Federal

Republic of Germany, Benelux states, Czechoslovakia and Poland. A number of 'indirect participants' were involved whilst France refused to participate at all. In total, the participants met some 46 times, without significant result.[1] However, the MBFR process did act as an important channel of communication between East and West helping to facilitate subsequent development of the CDE, CFE and other negotiating processes.[2] The failure of the talks was frequently attributed to disagreements over verification problems. Koulik and Kokoski assert that differences over verification were only a secondary explanation. They suggest primary responsibility for failure rested with the major variance in political and military considerations and interests between the parties during the course of negotiations in Vienna.[3] Eduard Shevardnadze, Soviet Foreign Minister for much of the period, cites fundamental differences over the nature and wider role of verification as a central feature in Soviet-US relations, even though he admits both sides utilised the issue of verification in their own propaganda war with each other.[4]

It has been suggested that serious advances in arms control could only be made when there was some convergence in the interests, perspectives, aims and objectives on conventional arms control between the participants, principally the Soviets and the United States. In Richard Falkenrath's study of the CFE Treaty he says that the actual convergence between the two sides was one of the most remarkable aspects of the whole process leading to the final agreement.[5] He proposes that the previous lack of progress was attributable to the lack of serious interest in arms control on the part of both NATO and the Soviets. NATO was said to be more interested in maintaining its force levels, whilst the Soviets wanted the West to participate in the CSCE process and add legitimacy to the territorial status quo within Europe. It is also suggested that advances in East - West arms control were also a means by which the West could better manage its straining defence budgets.[6] For the United States the MBFR talks provided the opportunity to negotiate troop reductions with the USSR so undermining Senator Mansfield's proposals to Congress for substantial unilateral US force cuts in its European based forces.[7] The combination of these divergent aims gave little incentive to the process of arms control, with little or no convergence between the wider aims of the two blocs.[8] This analysis is supported by Coit Blacker who also attributes the lack of progress within MBFR as there was no 'shared mutuality of interest'.[9] There is no evidence available at this stage to suggest any strength or coherence between the diplomatic groups involved sufficient to exert major collective influence on their own respective governments. The opposite is very much the case with national capitals driving the negotiation processes at the highest political levels.[10]

As well as problems posed by divergence in the wider aims there were also structural difficulties within the MBFR process itself. NATO had always held that WTO forces were much larger than its own and therefore an asymmetric reduction process on the part of the WTO would be required.[11] The geographic limit of the region covered by the talks also presented a significant restriction to the breadth of any agreement, in that the military considerations, even at theatre level, were of much wider significance to the whole of Europe rather than the extremely limited definition of 'Central Europe' that had been adopted for the MBFR talks. Connected to this was the expectation that a geographically limited agreement would do little to reduce NATO fears of surprise conventional attack.[12] On the issue of verification the two sides maintained fundamentally different pictures and assumptions on the actual size and character of the forces that were stationed in the region, and how they should be counted. The initial counting problems were never satisfactorily resolved, and for NATO representatives was an essential precondition for any eventual agreement. Thus the NATO participants quickly became convinced that there was no serious intent on the part of the Soviets to reach any meaningful agreement based upon comparable proposals in Vienna.[13]

Helsinki to Stockholm

In addition to the search for quantitative measures of arms control there have long been attempts to match these with more 'qualitative' initiatives, through confidence-building measures. The Helsinki Final Act produced a number of Confidence-building Measures (CBMs) as part of its 'Basket I' 'Conclusions on Aspects of Military Security'. Those measures were relatively modest and largely of a voluntary nature.[14] The agreed measures included provisions that required a 21 day pre-notification of large scale exercises and force movements involving over 25,000 troops within 250 kilometres of border areas. It also allowed for notification of smaller manoeuvres and the exchange of observers for large exercises.[15] However, these measures were not mandatory and the exchange of observers were to be arranged bi-laterally.[16] Most of the states sought to avoid agreeing actions that could detract from the recently commenced, and broader,

MBFR talks in Vienna. The Helsinki follow-up meeting at Belgrade in 1977-78 quickly demonstrated that there was little room for taking meaningful discussions on CBMs further forward because of the depth of disagreement between East and West.[17] There were constant antagonisms between NATO and the Soviet Union and WTO, with frequent allegations of violations of the existing CBMs that hindered and detracted from relations between the two blocs. The sober atmosphere of the Madrid follow-up meeting, which lasted nearly 3 years, between 1980-83, very much reflected the downturn in East-West relations following the Soviet invasion of Afghanistan. Again the Concluding Document of the meeting was rather thin, consisting mainly of a reaffirmation of the Helsinki Final Act with one exception. This was the agreement to commence a multi-stage Conference on Disarmament in Europe (CDE) to be based at Stockholm with the remit to discuss and develop measures that would provide early warning to diminish threat of surprise attack.[18]

Stockholm to Vienna

The Conference on Confidence and Security Building Measures and Disarmament in Europe, CDE, commenced at Stockholm in January 1984. The CDE process concentrated solely on the task of developing confidence and security building measures because of the continuing, but so far fruitless, MBFR negotiations in Vienna addressing arms control. By 1984 Soviet-US relations were so poor that the Reagan administration would only agree to the Stockholm talks on four conditions, which were heavily influenced by the French. First they had to remain under the CSCE umbrella and be part of a 'balanced process' that made advances in human rights areas too. The CDE and MBFR processes had to remain distinct ones. Again we can witness the distinction made between arms control and confidence building made by politicians and officials, despite their being conceptually linked. Finally, that the coverage on any negotiated measures be restricted to the European landmass and surrounding seas and airspace only - with the explicit goal of ensuring that their coverage was not extended to the United States.[19] Part of the agreed remit for the talks was that any agreement had to be of military significance, politically binding and contain adequate verification provisions. The negotiations were expected to last a long time and so were to be divided into 2 phases. Phase one would last from 1984 to the 1986 CSCE Follow-up scheduled to take place in Vienna, with phase two to follow on from that.[20]

The outcome of the measures agreed under the CDE were again relatively modest but strengthened considerably those contained in the Helsinki Final Act. The notification period for major movements and exercises was doubled to 42 days, whilst the size of notifiable activities were reduced to 13,000 troops. The invitation of observers to major exercises involving over 17,000 personnel became obligatory rather than voluntary. An annual calendar of military activities was devised to be circulated to other signatories, a year in advance. The final set of arrangements concerned rights of inspection upon other state's territories if they felt that compliance with the agreement might be in doubt. This permitted no more than 3 inspections per year to be made upon any CSCE state, with no more than one from any individual state. It was these challenge, On-Site Inspections that broke new ground in terms of verification processes and paved the way for similar measures in the INF and CFE Treaties. The Soviet change of position in agreeing to accept challenge inspections represented a major departure from previous Soviet policy and was a measure which they had consistently refused for the previous 40 years.[21] The effect of the 1986 CDE agreement was to very quickly dispel the fear of surprise Soviet attack of which NATO had complained for many years.[22] These advances were still relatively minor given the size of military forces deployed in Europe and in the scale of subsequent developments.

Moving the Impasse

It was not until April 1986 that the tenor of negotiations changed dramatically when Mikhail Gorbachev announced in East Berlin a new arms control initiative by proposing substantial reductions in certain categories of weapons and unit disbandments with the 'reduced' weapons either being destroyed or stored within national territories. This proposal went far beyond the remit of the MBFR talks by also calling for their abandonment as it was believed that they were unlikely to yield any agreement. The necessity for NTM and intrusive international verification measures, including OSI's, to ensure compliance, was also accepted as a possibility by Gorbachev in an announcement of April 1986.[23] As Richard Falkenrath suggests this announcement did not represent an immediate change in Soviet policy but it did indicate the increasing seriousness with which the Soviets were beginning to approach conventional arms control.[24] This was followed on June 11th 1986 when Gorbachev's initial proposal was enhanced with the 'Budapest Appeal' emanating from a Warsaw Pact summit meeting.

Vienna and the Leap Forward

When the third CSCE follow-up meeting in Vienna first convened in November 1986, the international atmosphere was radically different from that which had prevailed when the Madrid conference had begun. The change of Soviet leadership and its apparent high level commitment to renew the arms control efforts provided a largely optimistic backdrop to the discussions. The goals of the two blocs were reasonably clear from the outset. The East wanted notification and constraint provisions to be extended to independent air and naval activity, which it considered particularly important, whilst the West wanted to extend the OSI and data exchange processes of Stockholm much further.[25] However, generally the United States was reported as being 'luke warm' to the whole CSBM process and this affected the cohesion of the NATO stance bringing the US into conflict with other Alliance members.[26] For the neutral and non-aligned states the challenge was to try and get the two blocs to reduce the scope of their large military manoeuvres but they were themselves divided as to what the goals of the talks should be. One of the few things, however, upon which the three groups did appear to agree was that the CDE had not exhausted the possibilities for CSBMs to be further extended.[27]

More clearly the negotiation issues and processes would have to be different to those within the CFE process where there were disputes over certain categories of weapons or their deployment, with ceilings and holdings to be agreed and verified. The goals of the CSBM negotiations were to agree on a number of measures where the aims were of a wider, less tangible, nature.

The Development of Talks

Included in NATO's 1986 Brussels Declaration was the expressed willingness to engage in preparatory talks with the WTO on 'new' negotiations. These gradually developed into specific talks among the CSCE Delegation members from February 1987 on developing a specific 'CFE Mandate'. The US insisted the talks were kept out of the Vienna meeting and the French that they were informal. The agreed solution was that the G23 (NATO plus WTO members) states met weekly for a working breakfast at the embassy of a participating state and the content of the 'gypsy group' talks developed very quickly beyond procedural matters into substantive issues, very different from the stalemated formal Vienna discussions.[28]

The High Level Task Force report to NATO in 1986, which had been embodied in the Brussels Declaration, suggested that the gains of the recently concluded CDE talks in Stockholm be built upon and two separate negotiation processes begun:

- The 35 CSCE states to develop further the results of the Stockholm Conference.

- That the states whose relationship had the most direct bearing on military stability in Europe, namely the 23 members of WTO and NATO seek to eliminate disparities and establish conventional stability at lower levels.[29]

Thus the emphasis was clearly on maintaining two fora for discussions, but the link with the CSCE process was a controversial one. Whilst the French and most of the neutral and non-aligned states wanted the two sets of talks to take place together the US would have preferred for them to be clearly separated. The compromise was two different sets of talks within different parts of the Hofburg Congress Centre.[30]

But prior to any negotiations commencing a number of other issues had to be resolved between the two alliances over the objectives of the new talks, the items of equipment to be covered, participating states, the area of application and their relationship with the CSCE. On virtually all of these points the Warsaw Pact gave important concessions so that the talks that eventually took place very much conformed to Western preferences. These concessions tended only to come after WTO summit meetings or after personal intervention or involvement of Gorbachev or Shevardnadze to overcome inertia or opposition within the system. As Falkenrath phrases it:

The mid-level representatives in Vienna - many of whom were either military officers or Brezhnev-era holdovers were neither authorised or inclined to make the sort of concessions needed to meet NATO's demands.[31]

This again gives no indication of the influence of a trans-national epistemic community in arms control that could reach into the Soviet delegation in Vienna. What this view highlights is the attempt to de-privilege the Soviet military grip on arms control policy. Removing the military stranglehold allowed other sources of expertise and differing opinions to become available to Soviet decision-makers though they took time to reach Vienna. Thus change came about through rivalry between competing groups rather than through the emergence of epistemic 'agreement' within the Soviet system.

It was initiatives at the political level that drove the new Soviet positions, though they derived from a number of sources. However, those initiatives were themselves aided by new groups and individuals beginning to have greater influence over Soviet policy-making than had previously been the case. Institutions such as IMEMO and the Soviet Academy of Sciences were said to have been influential in the framing of some of Gorbachev's asymmetric reductions in his December 1988 speech. Thomas Risse-Kappen describes many of these internal developments as being due to the combination of domestic and transnational factors. A number of institutes and bodies had access to top Soviet decision-makers. ISKAN in particular had wider contacts with American and European bodies - Union of Concerned Scientists, Federation of American Scientists, Natural Resources Defence Council, SIPRI, Peace Research Institutes in Oslo, Hamburg and Frankfurt and others, which Risse-Kappen describes as a 'liberal internationalist community'. The contacts within this transnational community were fed to the Soviet leadership and became important in the framing of rapidly changing Soviet policy.[32] Individuals were also being invited by the Foreign Ministry to actively participate in the development of new strategy, though this was not connected with military work on arms control.[33]

Another explanation given for change in the Soviet arms control system was Gorbachev's broadening of the Defence Council to include lower field commanders and Shevardnadze. This broke the Soviet High Command's grip on the policy process, even though it was still serviced by the Defence Council Secretariat. The creation of the Politburo Arms Control Coordinating Committee (involving

KGB, Defence Ministry, Foreign Ministry, General Staff, Military Industrial Council and other departments) began to break the Defence Ministry's monopoly in the area.[34] That the initiatives at the Soviet centre were ahead of those of the Soviet delegation had a number of consequences. First that their Vienna negotiating delegations were frequently largely unaware, or at least without instructions, as to what the 'new' policies were. That the Foreign and Defence Ministries had very different, often rival and contradicting policy views, made it exceptionally difficult for Delegation officials to speak authoritatively about their government's policies. As a result, the delegation felt unable to work on its own authority to take advantages of new opportunities.

Pressures in the Soviet System

Mike Bowker has produced a useful synthesis of various explanations for the radical change in Soviet foreign policy during the 1980s that attempts to follow the change from a number of perspectives.[35] Whilst he asserts that internal reform in the Soviet system was relatively tentative until 1988 he suggests that in the foreign affairs field Gorbachev was both more active and successful. He says public pressure for foreign policy change was low and dismisses the role of the dissident groups and Mary Kaldor's argument about the effect of the unofficial Soviet peace movement.[36] Bowker stresses the importance of the slowing growth rate of the Soviet economy, the increasingly heavy burden of the Soviet military industrial complex and the lack of technological innovation and its lag behind the West as more important factors that indicated the necessity for radical reform. He says that this situation was exacerbated because of the disillusionment of the Soviet elite with the system. Brezhnev's 'stable cadre' policy had created frustration among the younger elements in the Soviet system denied promotion. Under Gorbachev the gerontocratic grip was loosened as forcible retirement and death took an increasing toll. It is suggested that the new Soviet leaders, having felt undervalued for many years wanted to make an impression, overcoming the effects of economic stagnation across all areas of Soviet society. They are also said to have perceived the West more as a model to learn from than as a threat.[37]

As well as the internal pressures the policies of the Reagan administration in particular created additional difficulties. The Kennan containment argument, when used in conjunction with a vigorous defence policy stance can be used as an explanation to account for the end of the Cold War occurring when it did by bankrupting the Soviet economy and military. Undoubtedly it created substantial pressures on the Soviet defence establishment but in the early years it appeared ready to try and meet these challenges. Bowker suggests that it was Gorbachev's reappraisal of Soviet defence policy in 1987 (a process that some argue commenced prior to Gorbachev) that began to minimise the Western threat that enabled the radicalisation of arms control policies as just one part of changes to all areas of Soviet military policy. Similarly the cost of maintaining and supporting Eastern Europe (economically and politically) was becoming just too burdensome for the Soviets to maintain.[38]

There is very little doubt that it was the qualitative differences between Soviet leadership under Gorbachev in comparison to his predecessors that allowed the enormous advances in the field of conventional and nuclear arms control. Whilst the motives for his different attitudes and behaviour may be open to interpretation their effect was to allow the reaching of agreements far beyond anything imaginable just a few years before. Prior to Gorbachev, Soviet arms control policy attempted to secure a number of goals. First, to protect the Soviet Union from conventional and nuclear attack from NATO. Secondly, to maintain Soviet dominance of Eastern Europe - euphemistically described as 'consolidating the gains of the Second World War'. A third objective was to prevent the resurrection of German power and fourthly to maintain the bi-polar international system. Those goals changed radically under Gorbachev's premiership.[39]

Gorbachev's perception of the necessity to restructure domestic economic and political elements of Soviet society was thought possible if it could be accompanied by a change to the Soviet role in the international system. A new arrangement with the West required a halt to be made to the arms race and a significant reduction in the military budget in order to free resources for domestic redeployment. To achieve any new arrangement with the West required the Soviets to look beyond traditional Cold War deadlock and the abandonment of some previously strongly maintained principles. These included changes that accepted that nuclear deterrence was unreliable and that the possibility of nuclear war was an acceptable risk. Security was not to be a purely military task, as maintained in the past, but it was a political responsibility resolvable by political means, with the role of the military changed from assuring triumph in the international class conflict to the prevention of war.[40]

'Reasonable Sufficiency' and the Internal Policy Debate

A partial explanation for changes to Soviet military doctrine is possible through the adoption of the 'reasonable sufficiency' concept, which was important both for the Soviets and NATO and which, according to Risse-Kappen, had its origins in the 'liberal internationalist community'.[41] For the Soviets the apparently deliberate vagueness of the concept was much debated because of the effect it would have on Soviet military doctrine. For the West too it meant trying to understand the effects that this would have on the structuring, deployment and operations of Soviet forces. As a concept it has political rather than military origins and can perhaps be best summarised as an attempt to stress the non-offensive nature of Soviet military doctrine, which had always greatly concerned the West. This meant abandonment of the necessity for numerical force superiority, but the maintenance of sufficient forces to halt and reverse any external attack upon it with a military structured in such a way that it did not pose a threat to other states. It accepted that asymmetrical reductions were possible so neutralising the 'competition strategy' and possibly indicated a greater openness to arms control verification than before. Internal Soviet debates between military and civilian representatives saw very different interpretations of the concept emerge and clearly indicated two very separate communities vying for position with little agreement between them. Gorbachev was unable to fully pursue his own particular policy preference because of the institutional power of the military which therefore required him at least to engage in the language of compromise.[42] Changes to Soviet military doctrine, uncomfortable as they were to many in the Soviet military, represented removal of another structural constraint on negotiations, reducing the breadth of events upon which the military could exert influence.

Adoption of these new principles allowed the Soviets to pursue a far more radical arms control agenda than was possible before. Both Gorbachev and Chief of Staff Sergei Akhromeyev hinted that conventional force asymmetries in the WTO's favour could be lessened by unilateral reductions to Soviet and Warsaw Pact forces. In return for these numerical reductions Gorbachev hoped that NATO would accept qualitative limits on some of its advanced and frequently superior military technologies. [43]

The radical agenda proposed by Gorbachev, his civilian advisers, Shevardnadze and his Foreign Ministry officials, were always likely to be strongly opposed by elements in the military command which under Brezhnev were used to having a major say in the overall aims and objectives of Soviet military policy.[44] Indeed by 1990 the differences between Defence and Foreign Ministries had become highly fractious with the Soviet General Staff becoming increasingly aggressive, undermining much of the new credibility that Soviet diplomats had gained in the previous few years.[45] Military officers were also concerned about their loss of power, prestige and future economic status that would result from large scale rapid force reductions producing widespread redundancies.[46] Oleg Grinevsky attributes much of the final success, within the Soviet system, in reaching agreement on CFE to political manoeuvering and the way that Generals Moiseyev and Akhromeyev were consistently outpaced by politicians.[47]

The economic pressures which faced the Soviet Union, and related arguments are often cited as the most powerful catalyst for change in the USSR and arms control policy.[48] Richard Falkenrath however, suggests that for the first time the presence of a mature civilian arms control team provided the Soviet leadership with a more independent and less self-interested source of advice than it had ever had from the Soviet military.[49] The combination of powerful economic pressures, high quality advice, a better understanding of the West and a military doctrinal re-evaluation made the Soviet desire for arms control more obviously serious than it had been since Khrushchev's attempts in 1960. Gorbachev's initiatives caught the West unprepared and suspicious of his motives and seriousness.

The Position of Non-Soviet Warsaw Treaty Organisation Members

The Warsaw Pacts negotiating positions were inevitably led by Gorbachev's, and other Soviet inspired initiatives. The Warsaw Treaty Organisation Political Consultative Committee established the Special Disarmament Commission (SDC) in May 1987 to co-ordinate WTO policy but up to the CFE mandate talks the smaller member states had little effect on the Soviet Unions negotiating position and priority was given to maintaining Pact solidarity rather than questioning Soviet rationale.[50] The political changes that began to sweep Central and Eastern Europe by 1989 rapidly undermined Soviet dominance, indeed the solidarity of the whole Organisation. However, the political tidal wave in Eastern Europe made very little difference to the final structure of the CFE Treaty itself because of some of its 'state based' design elements rather than sole dependance on alliance based structures.[51] The fracturing of WTO solidarity began to show itself tentatively at first, within the SDC, as Polish and Hungarian negotiators attempted to contribute to the formulation of common positions that were previously formulated only by the Soviets. The weakening of the SDC transferred more decision-making authority to delegations in Vienna though coordination between capitals and delegations was often poor.[52] These initial steps took some personal courage and negotiators risked national capitals revising their positions if the Soviets complained directly to them.[53] Hungarian Ambassadors Meister and Gyarmati were seen as prominent in disagreeing with the Soviets.[54] The fracturing of Soviet leadership and the WTO does not indicate the presence of any strong epistemic community among its members as, at least to start with, Jerzy Nowak says there was no possibility for links between like minded people.[55] That the Non-Soviet Warsaw Treaty Organisation   (NSWTO) delegations felt that they could take initiatives independently of their capitals - generally unusual behaviour for Ambassadors - it is unlikely that they would have done so without being sure of support from at least some of the other NSWTO Ambassadors or being certain that they could justify their actions on firm policy grounds. Though the top Soviet leadership was advocating a more autonomous role for the NSWTO members the same was not true at lower levels of the Soviet hierarchy - especially the military who wanted the WTO states merely to continue their unquestioning support for the Soviet position.[56]

French insistence that talks and force levels be conducted on a state basis had considerable effect as, particularly the Hungarians and Poles, began to loosen Soviet dominance.[57] Increasingly they began to define their own emerging strategic interests as the removal of Soviet forces from their territory and the whole of Central and Eastern Europe as the Hungarians in particular began to openly oppose WTO policy.[58] The increased preparedness of the top Soviet leadership to actually engage in 'real' discussion with other WTO states permitted these states, unusually, to have their concerns addressed on their merits and had a resultant influence on Pact negotiating positions.[59] The Hungarians and Poles increasingly began to combine their calls for the reform of the WTO into a voluntary consultative mechanism from a Soviet dominated military alliance, thus in the process distancing themselves from Moscow. As this happened the whole bloc began to lose its cohesiveness. Within the WTO Hungary and Poland were keen to embrace these Soviet economic and political reforms and wanted to go further. The Czechoslovaks and Bulgarians experimented with economic reforms but were reluctant to go further whilst the German Democratic Republic and the Romanians spurned all reform.[60]   Thus divisions in the Warsaw Pact had increasingly significant implications on the content and conduct of CFE negotiations rather than just the traditional East/West bloc discussions of the past. Indeed the simplicity of the inter-bloc negotiating arrangement was undermined as increasing Hungarian and Polish independence began to illustrate the extent of disunity within the Eastern bloc.[61] In 1990 the Hungarians announced the 'death of collectivity' within the Warsaw Pact, and agreed that they should meet no more as a group. The Poles, Czechoslovaks and Hungarians did begin to meet again separately to coordinate policy on a 'Visegrad basis'.[62] However, a UK delegation member counselled the Hungarians that too individualistic an adoption of this principle might mean that no agreement could be reached at all resulting in a loss for all participants.[63]

The Pace Quickens

The tenor of arms control activities entered another upward spiral in the December of 1988 when Gorbachev made a speech at the UN General Assembly. He announced the intention to withdraw some 50,000 Soviet troops and their equipment from Czechoslovakia, the GDR and Hungary and the demobilisation of a further 500,000 men by 1991.[64] This announcement was followed by considerable clarification and further developments in the succeeding months that demonstrated the magnitude of the unilateral reductions planned. They were to include the removal of a small number of Soviet nuclear weapons from Eastern Europe, and triggered all the other WTO members (except Romania) to initiate unilateral conventional reductions of their own whilst operating doctrine was to be restructured to make it less offensively based.[65] The idea of initiating deep unilateral reductions, no matter what the Western response, had been proposed in a radical article by civilian analyst Vitalii Zhurkin and two colleagues a year previously. Once articulated the idea became widely taken up by other civilian specialists, though unsurprisingly it met opposition from the Soviet Military High Command.[66]

The effect of these reductions on NATO were considerable. Initially they caught the West unprepared and sceptical of reductions on the scale ordered representing approximately 7% of WTO manpower in the Atlantic to the Urals area. In addition to the establishment of a domestic group known as GON (Public Monitoring of the Reduction of the Armed Forces and Armaments) headed by Andrei Kokoshin to monitor the changes, Gorbachev ensured that a US Congressional Group headed by Les Aspin visited the USSR and the GDR to see the reduction process for themselves. Although there were some concerns expressed by the US delegation over precise details they were very clearly able to see that the Soviet led measures were indeed genuine.[67] The most immediately observable effect was to make it clear that the Soviet Operational Manoeuvre Groups (OMGs) had been effectively emasculated. NATO had complained bitterly in the past that these Groups, based on large amounts of highly mobile armour, gave the WTO the ability to mount surprise attacks at very short notice and were cited by NATO as one of the main reasons why its members had to maintain high levels of defence spending.

The WTO reductions, in addition to the radical political changes in Eastern Europe, added weight to the domestic demands from within NATO states to cut their forces as a means to ease stretched defence budgets, in the face of a declining threat and increased warning time. Richard Bitzinger has discussed whether Gorbachev's unilateral reductions, between 1985-89, amounted to a GRIT (Graduated and Reciprocated Initiatives in Tension reduction) and offers some pertinent observations. He says that it took in excess of two years of unilateral Soviet actions before the West began to take them seriously. He asserts that the rapid rapprochement between East and West cannot be accounted for by adoption of a GRIT 'strategy' and his view is that it was probably the INF Treaty reached through traditional bargaining processes that helped to develop the perceived value of arms control processes - also showing that trust was not a pre-requisite for co-operation.[68]

1990 Vienna Document

There was considerable pressure from national capitals to try and find some agreement on CSBMs to take to the Paris Summit scheduled for November 1990. But at the fifth round of negotiations, between January 15-23 much time was spent on the Seminar on Military Doctrine. This Seminar which originated from a 1987 proposal, was a considerable success but the openness with which the NSWTO states were prepared to discuss military issues led to considerable discomfort for the Soviet delegation. However, there was some feeling that this Seminar was already out of date, not reflecting the political changes that had already taken place.[69]

The 1990 seminar was not a one off event, it represented the climax of a series of informal contacts that had taken place previously building up to the Seminar. These included informal meetings organised by SIPRI, the Pugwash Group and the Institute for East-West Relations and a semi-official meeting at Stiftung Wissenschaft und Politik at Ebenhausen in June 1989. Thus through such discussions the broadening of military contacts, beyond the political negotiating level and the articulation of national and alliance positions, postures and policies can be witnessed.[70] Another Military Doctrine seminar was held in October 1991 (provided for in the 1990 Vienna Document) and was reported as being much more in tune with changing military realities, where discussants presented details of how they were trying to reduce defence expenditures and challenges created by the introduction of modern technologies to the armed forces.[71]

It was relatively clear that some measures would be ready to present to the Paris Summit though their extent was likely to be problematic and complicated by the political processes unfolding in Eastern Europe. New suggestions for measures came thick and fast and old ones resurfaced. In February 1990 there were proposals to introduce a computerised communication system between the parties. NATO also proposed the exchange of information and the establishment of annual meetings to assess agreement implementation (representing institutionalisation within the CSCE), which had been proposed by the WTO in the previous year. In between sessions the UK proposed that peacetime visits to operational air bases be included and this was adopted in the next round. At Round 7 of the negotiations between May and November 1990 some other new proposals emerged which would allow 'unusual military activities' on a signatory's territory to be raised and subject to explanation and inspection.

Whilst the negotiations generally made good progress, there were a number of difficulties. The Soviets still had some anxieties about the ongoing negotiations on German unification during 1990, whilst the US seemed pre-occupied with the CFE negotiations. There was also the old Soviet interest in considering measures that would affect naval and air units whilst the Americans insisted they remained outside the remit for discussion. The Americans were relatively isolated on this matter as a number of other NATO delegations had no fundamental objections to the inclusion of information on naval forces.[72] It was also clear by September and October that a number of issues would not be resolved in time for the Paris summit and would have to be left over to the next round of negotiations planned for conclusion at the CSCE Review Conference in Vienna during 1992.[73]

Open Skies: Development of the Concept

The original idea of an Open Skies regime was first presented by President Eisenhower in July 1955 at a Geneva four power conference on surprise attack, where he proposed a mutual overflight regime, initially just between the USA and the USSR.[74] The time for such an agreement was not right in 1955 and it largely disappeared from sight until it was resurrected over forty years later. In May 1989, a speech by President Bush called for the revival of Eisenhower's original 'Open Skies' idea as part of a wider group of proposals calling for increased trust between East and West.[75] A meeting between Secretary Baker and Eduard Shevardnadze in September 1989 gave impetus to the idea and agreement to hold a joint conference on the idea.[76] The agreement that was finally reached in many ways demonstrates the fact that 'Open Skies' could not be easily accommodated within the CFE or CSBM negotiations. This has in many ways led to it being regarded as a somewhat lesser, hybrid and slightly 'specialist' measure often separated from the other measures.

The December 1989 Ministerial Session of the North Atlantic Council (NAC) issued a document that detailed some of the basic elements that it felt that any Open Skies agreement should embody as a development of Bush's May statement.[77] There was tension within the alliance over a number of issues about the prospects of Open Skies. For the US it was the first of the measures, then under discussion, that would directly affect its own territory. This led to US intelligence community assessments being prepared on the probable impact that an overflight regime would have on the American defence community. The by now standard concerns about Alliance structures surfaced - especially over the allocation of active inspection quotas with the US and Canadians being content to agree the allocation of the active quota within NATO whilst the French, supported by Italy and Spain, wanted national allocations to be pre-agreed.[78]   The NAC's final communiqué incorporated many of the elements that ultimately came to be written into the text of the Treaty. In the intervening months between the two statements Canada particularly had argued strongly for the development of such a regime. Canada's then External Affairs Minister, Joe Clark, was a major political force in urging pursuit of the issue arguing the many advantages he saw for all concerned.[79] His firm support also helped to ensure Canadian enthusiasm for the project and Canada's leading place within it.

The agreed international conference got underway in Ottawa in February 1990 but that and a further negotiating round in Budapest made little headway, producing only joint communiques that reflected the willingness to negotiate but little concrete progress.[80] Shevardnadze recalls that progress was largely blocked because of the more pressing nature of the prospect of German unification and the formulation of the 'two plus four' process.[81] The lack of progress was also attributed to the problems associated with two sides of a single problem. There was suspicion on the part of the Soviet Union about the degree of intrusiveness that NATO wished the regime to have whilst from NATO there was an insistence on the necessity for that degree of intrusiveness. The Soviet Union wanted to keep parts of its territory off limits, appeared concerned that NATO members might use prohibited sensors and so wanted to ensure that those sensors used would be very basic.[82] The Soviets also wanted to restrict overflights of Soviet territory to the sole use of Soviet aircraft and generally felt that the structure of the agreement would be of greater benefit to NATO than itself. NATO was determined that there should be no off limits areas and were unwilling to accept restrictions to use host nation aircraft only.[83]

Once the CFE Treaty was signed and German unification agreed there was a renewed interest in Open Skies and states were more inclined to invest political capital in it. This interest was again mobilized by Canada, encouraging the NATO allies to rethink their position on the proposals. The US had adopted some rather impractical positions concerning parts of the proposals but were susceptible to pressure from the allies especially given the incentive that it would permit the Americans to observe Soviet equipment moved East of the Urals - a problem causing difficulties within the CFE and the Article III dispute.[84] Full negotiations began again in September 1991 in Vienna. Successful conclusion of the agreement was speeded by the fact that the Russian negotiating team was much more positive than it had been prior to the abortive August 1991 coup, although the Soviet, then the Russian, military maintained its objections to the whole concept appearing happy to wrangle over technical issues so delaying conclusion.[85]

As with the CFE Treaty, agreement was only reached after considerable negotiation in the final phases with meetings continuously in the period 13th January into March 1992.[86] The sticking points revolved around a number of issues, mainly related to the allocation of costs and sensors issues which were not fully resolved and subsequently handed over to the Open Skies Consultative Commission to complete.[87] The final Treaty was signed by twenty five of the 30 CFE states.[88] Provision was also made for all the CSCE signatory states to accede to the Treaty upon application within six months of it entering into force. Special provision was also made for the accession of Soviet successor states.[89]

Negotiations and the Link to an Arms Control Epistemic Community

An analysis of the size and composition of national CSCE delegation sizes in Vienna during the period 1986-92 would provide some general observations and patterns.[90] Firstly that much of the fluctuation of state delegation size revolved around 3 key periods.

- The period leading up to the mandate talks.
- In the lead up to the CFE negotiations proper.
- After completion of the CFE Treaty.

The change in delegation sizes may well reflect to a large extent the perceived national interests at stake. Delegation sizes appeared to change with the phase of negotiations and their content. Overall there were large numbers of individuals involved in the stage of discussions up to the agreement of the CFE Mandate. After that the numbers fell but the proportions of delegations staffed by military personnel grew before commencement of the CFE talks proper and have remained at significantly higher levels than the pre May 1989 levels ever since.

In terms of state behaviour intra alliance disputes appear to have been of significance in affecting the size of national delegations. Within NATO disputes were largely handled within the HLTF and Quint, therefore delegation sizes maintained in Vienna reflect this. The United States multi agency approach, superpower status and primacy in Alliance leadership producing a delegation considerably larger than any of its partners. Of the other NATO states only the Turks experienced significant fluctuations in delegation size. Their fears about agreement borders, was reflected in a rapid growth in the size of its delegation during 1990. Even the French, with their insistence of the basis of state centred negotiation maintained a modestly sized delegation because many of its particular concerns could be addressed within the structure of the HLTF and Quint.

For the NSWTO states their relationship became increasingly fractious with the Soviet Union reflecting both change and decline in the Soviet Union. Those states most closely aligned to the Soviet Union, particularly the GDR, Bulgaria and Romania experienced minimal fluctuations until Soviet and WTO demise. During the same period the delegations of Poland, Hungary and Czechoslovakia appeared to grow reflecting their growing foreign policy independence. Even at this level of analysis this suggests that there is a hierarchy of leadership among the states which may have had some effect on the overall conduct of discussions. The relative consistency of overall delegation sizes and their composition, with the exception of the significant deviations explained above, may be indicative that these delegations have proved relatively impervious to external effects.

At a much more anecdotal level it is interesting to note the significant number of individuals who appear on delegation lists have also published work related to arms control and confidence building. These include S. Lehne (Austria), Lynn Hansen (US), Arie Bloed (Netherlands), P. Jones (Canada), Jennone Walker (US), Necil Nedimogolu (Turkey/NATO), H.G Van der Graaf (Netherlands) and P. Dunay (Hungary) among others.

When examining the implications of delegations in the context of networks and communities a number of features become clear. First, the relatively high turnover of staff appears to be indicative in most cases that few, if any, individuals' expertise is regarded as of such particular importance so as to require them to remain in Vienna for periods significantly longer than average posting times. This enables the significance of individuals within the arms control process to be questioned, showing a greater emphasis on the process rather than the role of any individual, and brings closer to the fore the possible importance of institutional affiliation. Given the significance attributed by Rhodes and Marsh and Martin Smith about the continuity of a limited number of actors, (though not necessarily individuals) this would suggest that, in their terms, conventional arms control is in fact a 'policy network' rather than a 'policy community'. The placing of individuals into diplomatic posts provides a well defined framework against which other state participants can undertake their own work providing formalised, ready contact and access points and framework for liaison. This enables the range of activities in which participants are involved to be defined, the range of possible national positions and policy options (policy enterprise) to be identified and the provision of a common vocabulary to emerge as discussion moves in an increasingly technical direction from the initial well understood form of diplomatic terms and associated meanings. In short it is a developing base for the socialisation of participants. These factors present a framework against which it may well be possible to establish the existence of an epistemic community. However, the role of individuals should not be totally overlooked. As Winner and McNerney observe the replacement of Stephen Ledogar, a diplomat, with James Woolsey, an arms control expert, as head of the US delegation in autumn 1989 was a signal to the Soviets that the Americans were prepared to speed up negotiations.[91]

Conclusions

This chapter has provided a relatively straightforward, perhaps in places over simplistic, picture of the changing environment for conventional arms control in the 1980s. From that examination a number of factors emerge that indicate why progress came when it did. First, the wider political environment, in which conventional arms control exists, was affected by major change at the international level. The arrival of Gorbachev and Shevardnadze facilitated real possibilities for progress even though support for them within the Soviet system was far from universal. It was not changes in the field of arms control *per se* that enabled the general improvement and relaxation in East-West relations. One British Vienna delegation member and CFE talks participant went so far as to say rapid progress in the negotiations were only possible for two reasons. First, the general improvement in Soviet-US relations and second, because of the rapid pace of wholesale political change within the Soviet Union itself.[92] Former Head of the Soviet CFE Delegation Oleg Grinevsky suggests that part of the reason why the initiatives were successful was that Gorbachev invested great political capital in CFE that helped to keep it at the top of the agenda. Bush, Baker, and Shevardnadze who attached similar importance to the process did likewise. Indeed so much attention was attached to negotiations that it almost created two sets of talks one at head of state and foreign minister level and the other at delegation level in Vienna.[93] These comments very much sum up the main reasons for progress, and how sufficient space was created at the international level for diplomats and technical experts to make progress towards agreement. It was not national or trans-national expertise that created the space for negotiation, it was interstate - but especially Soviet/US - political bargaining that made these agreements possible.

A second conclusion revolves around the issue of momentum. By the late 1980s it was clear that some East European states, particularly Hungary, Poland and Czechoslovakia, were increasingly beginning to adopt independent paths and devise and assert their own notions of national interest. Indeed the Vienna process gave these states a range of contacts that were useful in helping to establish and define elements of their increasingly independent policies. This coupled with the apparent fundamental change going on within the Soviet system itself made the need to reach agreement increasingly urgent. From the Soviet side, among other things, arms control would enable the diversion of scarce resources away from the military effectively curb their strength. On the Western side was a potential opportunity to limit the Soviets and effect defence reductions of their own. As the position became more and more parlous in 1989 and 1990 both East and West were increasingly determined to gain agreement before the structural changes left them behind. In short, each, with increasing urgency, was prepared to grant concessions in order to reach a quick agreement. Thus two distinct strands of pressure emerge. First the desire to reach an agreement on the size of conventional forces because bi-polar stability might disappear and multi-polar instability replace it. This made the prospect of reaching agreements that would address and minimize fears of military instability a very urgent and desirable goal. This was complemented by the second strand which meant that the imminent fracturing of the WTO was potentially going to make an agreement more difficult to reach, because of the increased numbers of parties that would be involved after its breakup.

Finally, what has not been clearly visible are forms of evidence that would indicate that a strong community actually exists in Vienna that significantly cuts across national and alliance boundaries. There is no strong evidence of a core group of individuals, based in Vienna, in the long term who have participated in arms control for a prolonged period. Indeed we have seen that it appears that it is largely national factors that have been primary in determining delegation size at various times during the negotiation processes.

The resulting agreements from the Vienna 'process' have generally been very successful. But the rapid conclusion of sometimes incomplete agreements, has brought with it a number of real and potential problems that have at times threatened to undermine them. The most significant of which has been the enormous regional change created by the dissolution of the Soviet Union and subsequent problems with its former constituent parts. Some of these problems will be pursued in more detail in the following chapter. But the overall result has been the creation of a network of agreements that lack some cohesion, and the creation of negotiation fora that only takes faltering steps without any real sense of direction. It is the lack of cohesion and absence of a realistic blueprint for the future that continues to pose the most serious structural problems to long term progress.

Notes

1   For a full discussion of the talks and the problems they encountered see J. Dean, (1987), *Watershed in Europe: Dismantling the East-West Military Confrontation*, (Lexington MA: Lexington Books).

2   J. Sharp, (1988), 'Conventional Arms Control in Europe', *SIPRI 1988 Yearbook: World Armaments and Disarmament*, (Oxford: Oxford University Press), p. 323.

3   S. Koulik and R. Kokoski, (1994), *Conventional Arms Control: Perspectives on Verification*, SIPRI, (Oxford: Oxford University Press), p. 78.

4   E. Shevardnadze, (1991), *The Future Belongs to Freedom*, (London: Sinclair-Stevenson), pp. 89-91.

5   R. Falkenrath, (1995), *Shaping Europe's Military Order: The origins and consequences of the CFE Treaty*, (Cambridge, MA: MIT Press), p. 1.

6   J.P. Rogers and P. Williams, (1994), 'The United States and CFE', *The Conventional Armed Forces in Europe Treaty: The Cold War End game*, S. Croft (ed), (Aldershot: Dartmouth Publishing), p. 88. Also F. Kupferschmidt, (1988), 'British and German Defence Co-operation at Sea and on the Northern Flank', *British-German Defence Co-operation: Partners within the Alliance*, K. Kaiser & J. Roper, (eds), (London: Jane's), p. 242.

7   J. Goldblat, (1994), 'Reduction of forces in Europe', *Arms Control: A Guide to Negotiations and Agreements*, (London: Sage), p. 171.

8   S. Koulik, and R. Kokoski, (1994), op. cit p. 78 and R. Falkenrath, op. cit. p. 3.

9   C.D. Blacker, (1988), 'The MBFR Experience', *US-Soviet Security Co-operation, Achievements, Failures, Lessons'*, (Oxford: Oxford University Press), p. 136.

10   M.R. Beschloss, and S. Talbott, (1993), *At the Highest Levels: The Inside Story of the End of the Cold War*, (London: Warner Books).

11   C. Bluth, (1990), *New Thinking in Soviet Military Policy*, (London: RIIA/Pinter), p. 96.

12   R. Falkenrath, (1995), op. cit p. 3.

13   Ibid. p. 4, for a more detailed description see S. Koulik and R. Kokoski, (1994), op. cit p. 80-81.

14   A. Bloed, (1993), 'Two decades of the CSCE process: from confrontation to co-operation', *The Conference on Security and Co-operation in Europe: Analysis and Basic Documents, 1972-1993*, A. Bloed (ed), (Dordrecht: Kluwer Academic), p. 47.

15   R. Freeman, (1991), *Security and the CSCE Process: The Stockholm Conference and Beyond*, (Basingstoke: Macmillan), p. 70.

16   D. Roberts, and C. Roberts, (1985), *How to Secure Peace in Europe*, (London: Harney & Jones), p. 88.

17   Ibid. p. 75.

18   A. Bloed, (1993), op. cit. p. 53.

19   J. Dean, (1987), *op. cit* 188-89. Also, J. Freeman, (1991), op. cit pp.85-88.

20   A. Bloed, (1993), op. cit p. 67.

21   J. Freeman, (1991), op. cit. p. 143.

22   V. Rittberger, M. Efinger and M. Mendler, (1988), *Confidence & Security Building Measures (CSBM): an evolving East-West security regime*, Tubinger Arbeitspapiers Zur Internationalen Politik Und Friedensforschung, Nr. 8.

23   S. Koulik and R. Kokoski, (1994), op. cit p. 88.

24   R. Falkenrath, (1995), op. cit p. 27.
25   J. Sharp, (1988), op. cit. p. 325.
26   J. Sharp, (1991), 'Conventional Arms Control in Europe', *SIPRI Yearbook 1991*, SIPRI, (Oxford: Oxford University Press), p. 452.
27   S. Lehne, (1991), *The Vienna Meeting of the Conference on Security and Co-operation in Europe, 1986-89: A Turning Point in East-West Relations*, (Boulder, Co: Westview Press), p. 67.
28   Ibid. p. 107.
29   J. Sharp, (1988), op. cit p. 331.
30   S. Lehne, (1991), op. cit p. 146-7.
31   R. Falkenrath, (1995), op. cit p. 30.
32   T. Risse-Kappen, (1994), 'Ideas do not float freely: transnational coalitions, domestic structures, and the end of the cold war', *International Organisation*, Vol. 48, No. 2, pp. 196-203.
33   G. Snel, (1997), 'Institutional Structure and Soviet Defence Policy Change', *Cooperation and Conflict*, Vol. 32, No. 2., pp.148-180.
34   J. Sharp, (1996), 'Changing Russian Attitudes Towards Conventional Arms Control', in K.M. Kelleher, J. Sharp and L. Freedman, (eds), *The Treaty on Conventional Armed Forces in Europe: The Politics of Post-Wall Arms Control*, (Baden-Baden: Nomos Verlagsgesellschaft), p. 86-7.
35   M. Bowker, (1993), 'Explaining Soviet foreign policy behavior in the 1980s', *From Cold War to collapse: theory and world politics in the 1980's*, Cambridge Studies in International Relations: 25, (Cambridge: Cambridge University Press), pp. 82-114.
36   Ibid. p. 98.
37   R. Falkenrath, (1995), op. cit p. 42.
38   M. Bowker,(1993), op. cit p. 105.
39   J. Sharp, (1993), *Soviet and CIS Perspectives on Conventional Arms Control*, Conference Paper: CFE and the future of conventional arms control, Kings College, 11-14 July, 1993, pp. 2-4.
40   C. Kennedy, (1994), 'The Soviet Union and CFE', *The Conventional Armed Forces in Europe Treaty: The Cold War Endgame*, S. Croft (ed), (Aldershot: Dartmouth Publishing), p. 42.
41   T. Risse-Kappen, (1994), op. cit p. 186.
42   See C. Bluth, 1990, op. cit p. 81-94.
43   Sharp, J., (1993), op. cit p. 6-8.
44   C. Bluth, (1990), op. cit p. 32-3, E. Shevardnadze, (1991), op. cit p. 147-48.
45   J. Sharp, (1993), op. cit p. 12.

46   C. Kennedy, (1994), op. cit p. 47-48.

47   O. Grinevsky, (1996), in K.M. Kelleher, J. Sharp and L. Freedman, (eds), *The Treaty on Conventional Armed Forces in Europe: The Politics of Post-Wall Arms Control*, (Baden-Baden: Nomos Verlagsgesellschaft), pp. 16-17.

48   M. Bowker, (1993), op. cit pp. 99-100. J. Sharp, (1996), op. cit p, 79.

49   R. Falkenrath, (1995), op. cit p. 37.

50   P. Dunay, (1993), 'Bargaining Behind the Curtain: Drafting the CFE Mandate - positions in the Warsaw Pact', Conference Paper: CFE and the future of conventional arms control, Kings College, 11-14 July, 1993, p. 5.

51   Though the CEE states still find the fact that they continue to be classified as part of a 'group of state parties' with the Russians tiresome.

52   J. Nowak, (1996), 'The CFE Regime and Its Development: A Polish and Central European Perspective', in K.M. Kelleher *et al*, p. 233.

53   Ibid. p. 230.

54   Ibid. p. 234.

55   Ibid. p. 230.

56   Ibid. p. 9.

57   Interview UK FCO official, October 1996.

58   J. Sharp, (1993), op. cit p. 376-77 and J. Nowak, (1996), op. cit p. 232.

59   P. Dunay, (1993), op. cit p. 9.

60   S. Lehene, (1993), p. 45 & 123.

61   Arms Control Reporter (1989), p 407. Box.196

62   Nowak, J., (1996), p. 232.

63   Interview with Canadian official, October 1996.

64   J. Sharp, (1990), 'Conventional Arms Control in Europe', *SIPRI 1990 Yearbook: World Armaments and Disarmament*, (Oxford: Oxford University Press), p. 460 provides a fuller description.

65   Ibid. p. 462-3.

66   B.S. Lamberth, (1992), 'A generation too late: civilian analysis and the Soviet military', in *Soviet strategy and new political thinking*, D. Leebaert & T. Dickinson (eds), (Cambridge: Cambridge University Press), p. 226, Fn. 32 & 33.

67   J. Sharp, (1990), op. cit p. 471-3.

68   R.A. Bitzinger, (1994), 'Gorbachev and GRIT, 1985-89: Did Arms Control Succeed because of unilateral Actions or In Spite of Them?', *Contemporary Security Policy*, Vol. 15, No. 1, p. 77.

69   J. Sharp, (1990), op. cit p. 503.

70   Ibid. p. 501 and J. Sharp, (1990), 'Conventional Arms Control in Europe', *SIPRI Yearbook 1990*, SIPRI, (Oxford: Oxford University Press), p. 503.

71   Z. Lachowski, (1992), The Second Vienna Seminar on Military Doctrine', Appendix 12B, *SIPRI Yearbook 1992*, SIPRI, (Oxford: Oxford University Press), p 496-505.

72   Borawski, 1991, op. cit. p. 71.

73   Ibid. p. 72.

74   W.W. Rostow, (1982), *Open Skies Eisenhowers Proposal of July 21, 1955*, (Austin: University of Texas Press), pp. 6-7.

75   Speech by President Bush, 12th May 1989, in L. Freedman, (ed), (1992), *Europe Transformed: Documents on the End of The Cold War*, (Tri-service Press: London), pp. 286-88, reproduced from *The Independent*, 13th May, 1989.

76   S. Koulik and R. Kokoski, (1994), *Conventional Arms Control: Perspectives on Verification*, SIPRI, (Oxford: Oxford University Press), p. 163.

77   L. Freedman, (1992), op. cit. pp.177-81.

78   S. Koulik and R. Kokoski, 1994, op. cit. p. 164.

79   R. Lysyshyn, (1992), 'Open Skies Ahead', *NATO Review*, Vol. 40, No 2, p. 23.

80   L. Freedman, (1992), op. cit pp. 192-3.

81   E. Shevardnadze, (1991), *The Future belongs to Freedom* (London: Sinclair-Stevenson), p. 133.

82   *Arms Control Reporter*, (1992), Box 409.

83   R. Lysyshyn, (1992), op. cit, pp. 23-4.

84   P. Jones and M. Krasznai, (1992), 'Open Skies: Achievements and Prospects', in J. Poole and R. Guthrie, (eds), *Verification Report 1992*, (London: VERTIC), pp. 48-9.

85   P. Jones, (1993), 'Open Skies: Events in 1992', in J. Poole and R. Guthrie, (eds), *Verification Report 1993*, (London: Brasseys/VERTIC), p. 148.

86   S. Koulik and R. Kokoski, 1994, op. cit p. 183. For a more extensive discussion of the negotiating process leading up to agreement see P. Jones, (1993), op. cit, pp. 145-152.

87   *Arms Control Reporter*, (1992).

88   The initial signatory states to the Treaty signed on 24th March, 1992 were Belarus, Belgium, Bulgaria, Canada, Czech Republic, Denmark, France, Georgia, Germany, Greece, Hungary, Iceland, Italy, Luxembourg, Netherlands, Norway, Poland, Portugal, Romania, Russia, Slovakia, Spain, Turkey, Ukraine, United Kingdom, United States. Kirgizstan acceded to the Treaty on 15th December 1992. Other Soviet successor states are permitted to accede to the treaty under special provisions made for Soviet successor states. Notably

Armenia, Azerbaijan and Moldova which all acceded to the CFE Treaty did not do so to the Treaty on Open Skies.

89   WEU, (1993), *Technical Co-operation in the framework of the Open Skies Treaty*, WEU Doc. 1364, (Paris: WEU), para 9.

90   K. Wright, (1998), *European Conventional Arms Control and Epistemic Communities*, PhD thesis, (University of Essex).

91   A.C. Winner and M.J. McNerney, (1996), 'Turning Points: The Link Between Politics and Arms Control', in K.M. Kelleher *et al*, 1996, p. 145.

92   Interview, British CFE Delegation member, October 1996.

93   O. Grinevsky, (1996), in Kelleher *et al*, 1996, pp.17-18.

3 The Institutional Network: Agreements and Procedures

This chapter takes a generalised perspective in looking at the main terms and provisions of the cornerstone agreements: the Conventional Armed Forces in Europe Treaty and supporting 'CFE 1A' agreement, the Treaty on Open Skies and the series of Vienna Documents. It does not attempt to provide a full description of the various agreements texts - these are widely available elsewhere. From the generalised descriptions of the main terms it seeks to show how the three link together and look at their respective institutional products, the Joint Consultative Group, the Open Skies Consultative Commission and the Annual Implementation Assessment Meetings and Forum for Security Cooperation as problem resolution mechanisms. It also highlights that whilst these agreements share a high degree of commonality they are far from seamlessly interlocking - a cause for some misunderstanding and frustration among practitioners.

The Conventional Forces in Europe Treaty (CFE)

Main Provisions of the Agreement

The CFE Treaty, signed in Paris on 19th November 1990 was, by any standards, a landmark agreement in conventional arms control. The terms of the Treaty were complicated, the text of considerable length to which were attached some eight additional protocols. Whilst it is unnecessary here to specify all the details of the Treaty, it is useful to summarise some of the main provisions.[1]

Participants. The agreement was signed by the 22 members of WTO and NATO. After the separation of Czechoslovakia both the Czech Republic and Slovakia added separate ratification's in 1993. The dissolution of the USSR saw the Russian Federation, Armenia, Azerbaijan, Belarus, Georgia, Kazakhstan, Ukraine and Moldova all later add separate ratification's bringing the total number of participants up to 30 when the Treaty was finally ratified by all state parties on 30th October 1992.[2]

Geographical area. The area of application covered all of the Atlantic to the Urals (ATTU), area from the Ural mountains and Caspian Sea in the East and including all the island territories of Europe out to the Azores in the West. Only part of Turkey is included as it is cut by a dividing line that runs from the 39th parallel to Muradiye, Patnos, Karayazi, Temen, Kemaliye, Feke, Ceyhan, Dogankent, Gozne and then on to the sea. Within that area there were 3 centrally defined zones and a flank zone each with their own specified sub-limits. The Treaty specified numerical limits for some five categories of weapons: Main Battle Tanks (MBT's), Armoured Combat Vehicles (ACV's), Artillery, Combat aircraft and attack helicopters. Any excess of this 'Treaty Limited Equipment' (TLE) was to be destroyed, 'cascaded' to other states or converted to alternative uses.

Reduction Provisions

Treaty Provisions meant that holdings of equipment above agreed limits that was not to be 'cascaded' (transferred) to other states had to be disposed of or converted in strictly specified ways. The alternatives included; destruction, conversion to non-military purposes, static display, use as ground targets, modification, ground instructional purposes, reclassification or recatergorisation.[3] 'Look-a-likes' posed difficult problems for inspection and verification as they are excluded from the Treaty. 'Look-a-likes' are those items of equipment such as some field ambulances and communication vehicles that externally resemble (often close to identical) items of TLE like armoured infantry fighting vehicles but which are not combat capable. Such items require particularly close inspection to ensure their operators are not evading Treaty restrictions and it was an issue, which at least initially, proved troublesome.

The protocol on destruction specified that equipment could be severed, subjected to explosive demolition, deformed, smashed or converted to target drones. The expectation was that little equipment was likely to be destroyed because states had found numbers of 'ingenious ways in relocating, converting and recatorgorizing equipment'.[4] For example 'conversion to non-military purposes' might mean that some tanks could be turned into heavy bulldozers, power units, rescue and casualty evacuation transports. The 'reclassification' option might mean that combat aircraft be converted to unarmed trainers by the removal of internal weaponry and the facility for carrying external stores. Combat helicopters could be converted to 'combat support helicopters', which are not covered by the Treaty, by the removal of internal and external weaponry and integrated fire control and aiming systems. Such conversion to be previously notified and the end result verified by inspection. Of course the concern remains that equipment that may be converted or reclassified can, in most circumstances, be reconverted again at a later date if desired. Thus there is not a dedicated goal of equipment destruction but an opportunity within the Treaty for the effects of the agreement to be reversed, even though it might be an expensive process, if the participants felt that the usefulness of the Treaty was reduced at some later date. Therefore a situation is created where states can hedge a current restriction on their military capabilities against the possibility that they might be required again in an uncertain future. Similarly 'cascading' ensured that the most modern equipment could be retained, particularly within alliances, by passing it onto other members.

Treaty Protocols

In addition to the main Treaty text its 8 supplementary protocols covered:

- Existing Types of Conventional Armaments and Equipment.
- Procedures Governing the Reclassification of Specific Models or Versions of Combat-Capable Trainer Aircraft into Unarmed Trainer aircraft.
- Procedures Governing the Reduction of Conventional Armaments and Equipment Limited by the CFE Treaty.
- Procedures Governing the Categorisation of Combat Helicopters and the Recatergorisation of Multi-purpose Attack Helicopters.
- The Notification and Exchange of Information.
- Inspection methods and procedures.
- The establishment and operation of the Joint Consultative Group.
- The Provisional Application of certain provisions of the full Treaty.

The agreement was to be implemented in 4 phases which were to be completed within 40 months of it coming into force.

Phase One: A baseline validation period of 120 days to allow the gathering and exchange of data for verification purposes.

Phase Two: The reduction phase of 3 years to cover the destruction, conversion or 're-certification' of equipment.

Phase Three: The Residual Level validation of another 120 days to confirm post reduction data.

Phase Four: Of unlimited duration where there would be continued inspections to check on data and continuing compliance with the agreement.[5]

The complexity of the Treaty itself and the extensive protocols very much reflect the lack of trust between the parties involved - mainly directed against the Soviet Union. The complexity and close definition of verification provisions reflected the previous absence of generally agreed definitions and terms prior to the CFE negotiations. The lack of mutual trust by the participants is particularly reflected in the comprehensive nature of the verification regime developed to ensure compliance with its terms.

One noticeable feature of the eight protocols and the completion of the four implementation phases was that they are largely left in the hands of military officials and experts rather than being explicitly retained by diplomats and politicians, although there are undoubtedly opportunities for both to become re-engaged in the process through the Joint Consultative Group when problems are unresolved between military officials.

Joint Consultative Group

The JCG was established under Treaty protocol to deal with Treaty compliance and possible circumvention, resolution of ambiguities and differences of interpretation, measures to enhance the Treaty, the updating of lists of current equipment, resolving differences and working methods on inspection procedures. The JCG also has the facility to propose amendments to the Treaty and undertake the organisation of any extraordinary meeting of the signatories and the Treaty Review Conference (Treaty Text, Article XVI). Conferences unlike the JCG itself could adopt substantial amendments to the Treaty. The Protocol on the JCG, specified in Article XVI, detailed that there were normally to be two meetings per year, of no longer than 4 week duration, and extraordinary meetings as required. It also specified a variety of routine administrative procedures for the Group's operation. Decisions within the Group were to be taken by consensus and its proceedings and findings confidential.

The frequency of JCG meetings has been much higher than the Treaty protocol laid down. Within the JCG, in addition to the weekly plenary sessions, there are a number of separate working groups that deal with specific issues.[6]

The purpose of the JCG has also been described as more than just a means to resolve disputes but a mechanism through which the agreement can remain flexible in a rapidly changing Europe.[7]

The great strength of the JCG is its extremely narrow focus which requires a high degree of professionalism from those involved and allows core issues to be very quickly thrown into stark relief. Issues cannot be blocked from discussion, even if agreement cannot be reached. Particularly persistent issues are likely to attract media attention, via judicious leaks, despite the strong confidentiality conditions that are applied to the Groups operation. Falkenrath also describes the JCG as the location where the high level pledges of participants are translated into action and where the success of that translation can be monitored and details fed back to national capitals.[8]

Experience of JCG Operations

The experience of JCG operations has been considerably different from that specified in the Treaty - extending it somewhat beyond the minimalist remit that Treaty language outlined. It was reported in 1992 that the JCG had been in almost continuous session since the signing of the Treaty. The dissolution of the Soviet Union was creating serious problems for ratification of the agreement both at a practical level and at the level of international law with most delegates to the JCG wanting to 'lock in' the agreed cuts by rapid ratification with other issues to be dealt with separately.[9]

Concern over the reported figures of Soviet equipment in the initial Treaty data exchange were the most pressing issue to be dealt with in the JCG. The first meeting of the JCG, which started just 11 days after Treaty signature, running until 13th December and then reconvening in January 1991,[10] dealt with, among other things, a clarification of why the Soviets had markedly reduced the numbers of Objects Of Verification (OOV) which created discrepancies between US intelligence estimates and Soviet disclosures.[11] These issues were also pursued outside the JCG particularly by meetings between senior American and Soviet official and politicians.[12] These problems were resolved in 1991 by the Soviets submitting revised force estimates in May and in a statement to the JCG in June the Head of the Soviet JCG Delegation agreed that the Soviets would destroy some of the equipment that had been moved East of the Urals, use some of it for replacement purposes and store the remainder.[13]

In 1994 the continued weekly frequency of JCG meetings continued. Although the JCG does not publish reports of its own, some insight into the issues discussed there have been gleaned from reports to national parliaments. For example the US ACDA complained that Soviet states had denied Western inspectors access to sites in Russia, Ukraine and Belarus whilst a number of others had submitted inaccurate or incomplete data.[14] Problems of other newly independent former Soviet states appeared to have been treated more sympathetically. With ongoing conflict in Armenia and Azerbaijan CFE inspectors were unable to verify holdings and/or any reductions, but appeared apparently relaxed about the problem because much of the old Soviet equipment was no longer operable, suggesting that the situation could be remedied by more careful accounting at the end of phase two.[15]

Another important complaint was the high cost of the very expensive destruction procedures agreed within the Treaty that was making compliance very costly for them. The JCG agreed to investigate other methods but Western officials were wary that destruction methods should not become degraded to permit them to be reversible.[16] Eventually after negotiations the issue was finally resolved in July 1993 based upon Russian and German discussions[17] whereby armoured vehicles could be destroyed by crushing using a large compactor, though this was still felt by the Russians to be too expensive.[18]

CFE Compliance Record

The CFE Treaty has faced 2 significant challenges to its operation. The first, briefly outlined above, emerged almost immediately upon signature of the Treaty relating to inspection quotas, was then resolved fairly quickly.

However, the second challenge over the 'flank problem' has proved much more difficult to resolve and on a number of occasions has almost threatened to totally undermine the agreement. The problem again emerged soon after Treaty signature as Russia's strategic environment radically changed. It centres upon the difficulties created for the Soviet Union, and subsequently Russia, and to a lesser extent Ukraine, on the limits imposed on the levels of forces stationed within the zones created by the Treaty.

The zoning arrangement of the Treaty was an attempt to limit the concentration of military forces in central Europe. On NATO's part there appeared to be no strong desire to create specific sub-limits on the flank zone, whilst the WTO states wanted zonal limits established to prevent the Soviets from relocating forces close to their countries then being withdrawn from the Central European zone. Despite Soviet sensitivities a number of proposals were agreed that established equipment ceilings and storage arrangements on the flanks although they were not to become effective until November 1995. As the

WTO limits in this peripheral zone also included Romanian and Bulgarian forces the actual amounts of equipment that the Soviets could hold was actually quite small.[19]

The creation of Armenia, Azerbaijan, Georgia, Ukraine, Moldova and the Russian Federation meant that the Treaty Limited Equipment (TLE) holdings now had to be shared between six states and not held by just one, thus considerably reducing the flexibility for deployment that the Russian military sought. The final allocations under the Tashkent agreement meant that approximately half of the flank zone holdings were in the hands of Armenia, Azerbaijan, Georgia and Moldova, with the remaining half then sub divided between the Ukraine and Russia. Not only this but a proportion of the equipment that remained had to be kept in storage and could not be held by active units.[20] During 1992 and 1993 the problem became even more serious for the Russians as warfare between Armenia and Azerbaijan, internal strife in Georgia and conflict in Moldova developed. All of this hampered Russian withdrawal and caused some to question whether it should be doing so at all.[21]

On the Northern flank the position was somewhat different. The withdrawal of Russian forces from Non-Soviet WTO states in Eastern Europe, coupled with the removal of troops and equipment from Soviet successor states, created the need to re-deploy considerable amounts of men and materiel. The CFE flank limits meant that the relatively well developed military infrastructure in the old Leningrad Military District could not be fully utilised thus creating a need for the construction of new military complexes elsewhere within Russia.[22]

In early 1993 Russian unhappiness with the flank limits surfaced again after General Grachev visited military units in the Caucasus and this dissatisfaction came to be repeated many times, particularly at bilateral meetings with US officials.[23] At that time Russian forces were stationing an approximate 50% excess of TLE above agreed limits in the flanks zone.[24] Western states made it clear that they did not want major revisions to the Treaty even after Yeltsin made an appeal to the major Treaty signatories in September 1993. He presented reasons to support revision, that described Russia's fundamentally changed security position, the increased significance of the 'Southern arc' to Russia and the social and economic tensions it was likely to create within the military.[25]

At a Joint Consultative Group meeting in September 1993, Russia formally proposed suspension of Article V. Not surprisingly this was adamantly opposed not only by the Turkish and Norwegian delegations but most other

Western delegations too. There was also the expectation that once one change was agreed a number of other demands for revision were likely to follow from the Russians.[26] The Ukraine supported Russia's request for Article V suspension because it would have allowed the Ukraine to reorientate its forces away from the Western part of the country to the East.

The dispute continued into 1994 and the situation worsened considerably with Russian intervention in Chechnya. In April of 1995 Pavel Grachev confirmed that Russia would not be able to comply with the terms of Article V while Chechen unrest continued. At the May 1996 Review Conference in Vienna, agreement was reached to reduce the size of the flank zone, the granting of a 3 year transition period to allow the new limits to be met. Russia was also to 'borrow' some of the quotas of TLE from Georgia and Armenia for the purposes of counting equipment.[27] This 'temporary borrowing' of excess quotas, and practice of 'temporary deployments' has been both unpopular and was clearly unsatisfactory in providing a permanent resolution to the problem.

Despite the seriousness of the problem it could not be resolved. As no acceptable political solution was found the flank issue was deferred from full discussion via variety of short term mechanisms, accompanied by pledges to look at CFE 'adaption' as soon as possible. The West could not see the provisions abandoned without the possibility that the entire agreement might be lost altogether, whilst the Russian political leadership could not be seen openly to be incapable of adhering to an important international agreement or lose face to the Russian military so completely. The promises of full CFE adaption given at the Lisbon OSCE summit were reiterated as part of NATO-Russia Founding Act signed in May 1998 and finally reached a conclusion in the September 1999 OSCE Summit - almost 8 years after the problem first emerged.[28]

The Vienna Documents

The negotiations on conventional 'arms control' were kept separate from issues of 'confidence building' within Europe during the 1970s and 1980s for practical reasons, outlined below, though analytically it is much more difficult to treat the two areas separately. Indeed many would argue there is an almost organic link between them, and that to try and develop measures in one area without advances in the other would be extremely difficult.

In practical terms the talks were kept separate because of the American desire to keep MBFR, for which it had little enthusiasm, separate from the CDE process. In the follow-on there were disputes, particularly with the French, on keeping the G23 of NATO and the WTO separate from the G35 of the CSCE and whether they took place on an Alliance basis or that of state parties. Whilst the negotiations were kept separate and the MBFR process maligned, many of the proposals that came to be incorporated in the CDE agreement and the Vienna Documents had their origin within the 'Associated Measures' section of the MBFR talks.[29] The largely overlapping nature of the CFE and CSBM negotiations is illustrated by John Borawski's statement that:

> Were it not for the 12 neutral and non-aligned European CSBM participating states all the CSBM proposals could just as easily been treated as CFE stabilising measures, thus questioning the very raison d'être of the CSBM negotiations as a separate forum...[30]

The 1990 Vienna Document was superceded by the 1992 and then the 1994 Document. This Document has formed the definitive agreement to date to which other clarifications and further measures agreed within the FSC have been annexed.

Main Provisions of the Agreement: The main measures covered provisions relating to the exchange of military information, information on the deployment of new weapons system, defence planning information, consultation and cooperation on unusual military activities, programmes of military contacts, notification and observation of certain military exercises and activities, calenders of activities, constraining provisions, and inspection and evaluation arrangements (including annual implementation meetings).

Participants: As the map of Europe changed during the 1990s so too did the number of participants to include: Albania, Armenia, Austria, Azerbaijan, Belarus, Belgium, Bosnia-Herzegovina, Bulgaria, Canada, Croatia, Cyprus, the Czech Republic, Denmark, Estonia, Finland, France, Georgia, Germany, Greece, the Holy See, Hungary, Iceland, Ireland, Italy, Kazakhstan, Kyrgyzstan, Latvia, Liechtenstein, Lithuania, Luxembourg, Malta, Moldova, Monaco, the Netherlands, Norway, Poland, Portugal, Romania, the Russian Federation, San Marino, Slovakia, Slovenia, Spain, Sweden, Switzerland, Tajikistan, Turkey, Turkmenistan, Ukraine, the United Kingdom, the United States of America, Uzbekistan and rump Yugoslavia with a delegation from the former Yugoslav Republic of Macedonia attending meetings as an observer from 1993.

Geographical Area: The geographical area of application is defined in the Vienna Documents as:

> ....the adjoining sea area and air space is concerned, the measures will be applicable to the military activities of all the participating States taking place there whenever these activities affect security in Europe as well as constitute a part of activities taking place within the whole of Europe as referred to above, which they will agree to notify. Necessary specifications will be made through the negotiations on the confidence and security-building measures at the Conference.[31]

The 1990 Vienna Document

The 1990 Vienna Document contained a number of measures that refined provisions in the 1986 CDE agreement with a number of, at that stage modest, but nevertheless important innovations. It has the status of a politically binding document, in the same vein as previous and subsequent agreements, rather than as an international Treaty. Main changes included that the annual exchange of information contain data on current and projected military budgets and details on the planned deployment of new weapons systems, data about the size and strength of units and their equipment to be reported every December. There was also agreement to step up the programme of military contacts, particularly with airfield visits. This CSBM agreement also contained an implicit right for states to conduct intra-alliance inspections, a right which the Hungarians asserted, with Czechoslovak and Polish support in an interpretative statement attached to the agreement.[32]

    Another important element was the introduction of a computerised communication system, to be co-ordinated by the Netherlands which although elementary in technological terms, would provide the possibility for 24 hour contact and the exchange of information to complement diplomatic channels.[33] Of potentially considerable importance was the creation of the Conflict Prevention Centre (CPC) which was formally established via the Charter of Paris. Its function was to oversee the implementation of CSBMs, particularly in regard of the provisions concerning the notification of 'hazardous incidents' and 'unusual military activities'. It was also to manage the new communications network and support the required Annual Assessment Implementation Meetings (AIAMs).[34]

1992 Vienna Document

The 1992 Vienna Document represented the end of the rapid phase of the CSBM negotiations with subsequent agreements being more incremental in nature. The 1992 Document incorporated all the measures within the previous agreements filling out still further the provisions of the 1990 Vienna Document. By this time the number of signatories had grown too, from 35 to 48 with the accession of Soviet and Yugoslav successor states.[35] With violent conflicts raging in Yugoslavia and along the periphery of the former Soviet Union the limited value of the existing CSBM system, that had evolved between the two blocs, was clearly demonstrated.[36]

The amount and detail of information required in the annual exchange of information increased considerably. It was particularly true in the case of data concerning units that are maintained at reserve or cadre level to be activated and reconstituted during mobilisation. This was an issue that had not been seriously addressed previously. The major objector to these provisions were the Swiss who would not accept compromise unless the thresholds were kept sufficiently high to ensure that their training exercises were not 'captured' by these provisions.[37] In relation to the deployment of new weapons states had to provide specified information and photographs, and in some cases demonstrate them, to the other participating states. There was also the requirement to provide information on APC look-a-likes, which had, and were, posing problems for CFE inspectors.[38] The voluntary hosting of visits was institutionalised, to permit states in areas of tension to invite accredited individuals such as military attaches to view activities in the affected area.[39] The threshold levels of personnel and equipment which would generate notification were again lowered and the liability to observation of major activities was increased. Table 3.1 illustrates how the notification observation regimes have changed since the Helsinki Final Act. A number of 'constraining provisions' prevented states from undertaking more than one activity every two years that involved more than 900 tanks or 40,000 troops. They also restricted the number of smaller activities that could be held simultaneously or in a specified period.[40]

Table 3.1: Changes to the Vienna Documents Notification Regime

Agreement	Notification	Size	Observation
Helsinki Final Act 1975	Voluntary 21 days in advance	20,000 troops	Voluntary on bi-lateral basis
Stockholm Conference on Disarmament in Europe 1986	Compulsory, 42 days in advance	13,000 Troops 300 battle tanks 3000 amphibious/ paratroops 200 fixed wing sorties	17,000 troops or 5,000 amphibious/ parachute drop
Vienna Document 1990	as above	as above	as above
Vienna Document 1992	as above	9,000 Troops 250 battle tanks 3000 amphibious/ paratroops 200 fixed wing sorties	13,000 troops or 3,500 amphibious/ parachute drop 300 battle tanks
Vienna Document 1994	as above	as above plus 250 artillery pieces, or 500 ACV's	as above plus 250 artillery pieces, or 500 ACV's
Vienna Document 1999	as above	as above	as above

Verification and Evaluation Elements of the Vienna Documents

Because there is no firm baseline, holdings or reductions to be verified as in the CFE agreement the 'verification processes' such as they are of a very different nature. There is again an information exchange mechanism, broad in outlook, which allows participants to evaluate, in detail, the data provided and to compare it with national or other estimates. There are provisions that permit visits to active and inactive units to allow the information provided about them to be validated, within overall ceilings specified in the agreements.[41] The visit and contact programmes, though mandatory in some cases, are relatively modest such as the provision for visits to airbases for which no state is expected to host more than one visit in a five year period.[42] For wider contacts such as exchange visits, joint sporting activities, making places available on command and training courses to other nationals have no quantitative or qualitative values specified.[43]

At a 1995 Seminar on the OSCE experience in confidence-building, the importance of the contact and visit programmes was said to have a benefit far greater than the observation of equipment and activities to which they formally relate as

> The broader understanding developing from informal discussions and appreciations gained during the course of inspection visits was of a substantial value in itself ....[44]

The concept of the challenge inspections has been improved, though no state is obliged to accept more than 3 such inspections in one year, but it cannot refuse the inspection and the inspecting state can specify the area to be visited. However, access within the area to be inspected is not unrestricted and inspected states can declare some areas 'sensitive'.[45] The balance of authority on restricting access rests very much with the host state though clearly apparent unreasonable denial to access would undermine the purpose of confidence-building.

Annual Implementation Assessment Meetings

The creation of Annual Assessment Implementation Meetings (AIAMs), originally conducted under the guise of the Consultative Committee of the CPC, now part of the FSC, are in effect plenary sessions at which the clarification or explanations sought or proffered on previous activities and the information exchanged, also for compliance problems to be raised. The first AIAM was held in Vienna on November 11-13th 1991, though publicly available data concerning its discussions is not readily available, it has been reported that there were no major discrepancies, though some interpretations were resolved after 'frank' discussions.[46] The November 1992 AIAM was reported as a less heated affair with participants drawing up a list of recommendations to improve and harmonize existing measures.[47] It highlighted an emerging problem which was the rush to produce measures under the Vienna Documents, the CFE Treaty and Treaty on Open Skies had produced inefficient, duplicating or conflicting measures which needed fairly prompt revision. The April 1993 AIAM produced similar outcomes but there was an increased awareness that notification thresholds for military exercises be reduced further to capture the generally smaller character of military exercises of the 1990s.[48]

As has been previously mentioned there is normally considerable secrecy over the operation of the FSC but access to the summary Journals for the 1994 AIAM provides some interesting observations on the extent of participation in the CSBM process. Journals from the 3 days of the meeting show very much that it was a working affair with agenda items dealt with by discussion groups presented by a moderator.[49] The modalities and style of the meeting having previously been agreed at the FSC meeting on 9th March 1994.[50] From the discussion of the results of the AIAM was the expression of regret that not all of the participating states attended the meeting and that less states than previously were participating in observation and airbase visits. Concern was also expressed over the failure by many states to provide annual information by the due date. Again a number of proposals were made by the Delegates on improvements that could be made to the Vienna Document.[51] The OSCE report on the 1995 AIAM is uninformative but suggests that more time was to be devoted within the FSC to ensure implementation of the existing agreements.[52]

By 1997 the calls for more public transparency in the process were beginning to have an effect with more details of these meetings becoming available to a wider public audience with the publication of some FSC documents and AIAM Chairman's reports. By the time of the 1999 AIAM a pattern of perceived weaknesses in the Vienna Document was becoming clear producing a familiar agenda for discussion. These included:

- Problems in ensuring that all states exchanged information required under the Vienna Documents, its format and synchronisation with the requirements of the agreement on the Global Exchange of Military

Information.
- The fact that some states were still not connected to the OSCE Communications system and its high cost of operation for some states.
- The low total inspection quota and its asymmetric application. The inspection quota under the Documents is relatively small and this tends to be almost totally used in the first quarter whilst very few inspections take place in the remainder of the year.
- Some states laggardly application of the scheduling of visits and participation in the programmes of contact.[53]

Compliance Record

In the overall context of their design implementation of the Vienna Documents has generally been successful, but has also greatly benefited from the more cooperative atmosphere from 1988/89 onwards facing little real test of their effectiveness. Equally the decline of their applicability in an evaporated Cold War scenario, even though notification and observation thresholds have been lowered, means that they lost some of their value. This is especially true in the case of the disintegration and conflict that has surrounded the former Yugoslavia. Their dependence on a state based design has proved to be inadequate demonstrating some major shortcomings in a radically changed Europe.

The demise of the Soviet threat and then the Soviet Union itself, has helped shift the immediate interest in CSBM application much further Eastwards. Although still important in the 'West' their significance to some states has declined, but to successor states of the FSU and for Central and East European states have, if anything, increased. However here the records of participation and compliance are much more complicated than in the West. Compliance with the agreed procedures and arrangements has generally been high - except in cases of ethno-nationalist conflict - but participation in actual discussions by the smaller Soviet successor states in particular is relatively low.

The increasingly comprehensive and complicated nature of the CSBM regime has also increased the probability of technical violations of the accords; such as with Russian and CIS non-supply of data on planned military activities for 1993 by the December deadline. Conflicts in Georgia, Moldova, Armenia and Azerbaijan all posed difficulties for CSBM implementation - as it has for the application of the CFE Treaty and CFE-1A agreement. Although no major breaches or circumventions have been reported, the extremely rapid accession to agreements by FSU successor states in 1990 and 1992, many of whom did not even participate in the negotiations, has produced a number of technical violations.[54] The violations that have taken place are largely unrelated and unsystematic, indicating more that most FSU states lack effective mechanisms available to monitor their commitments, obligations and the progress of their own compliance rather than deliberate evasion.[55] But the problems of technical violation continue to persist.

For states lacking the infrastructure to collect and analyze data concerning their military forces it is important that steps are taken, and where necessary continued assistance given, to ensure such deficiencies are remedied. The importance of this can be seen in retrospect where events such as the Yugoslav failure to provide the required military data in December 1991 should have given some early indication of the re-grouping going on within the Yugoslav military for potentially aggressive purposes.[56]

Treaty on Open Skies

Main Provisions of the Agreement

This international Treaty signed in March 1992 contains important provisions for states to combine and form 'Groups of States Parties' for the purpose of Treaty implementation.[57] Initially Belgium, the Netherlands and Luxembourg, but also Russia and Belarus combined to form two such groups. This permits the sharing of active and passive inspection quotas between them. Such a decision also offers considerable scope for cost sharing, by pooling aircraft, sensors, personnel, processing and interpretation costs etc.

Parties to the agreement are allocated a quota to both undertake flights as an 'observing party', the 'active quota' and a quota of flights which they must be prepared to receive, the 'passive quota', as the observed party. These quotas were established by negotiation, and a provisional allocation of quotas for each of the first three years after the Treaty fully enters into force, agreed. These can be subject to changes, for example, if states agree to combine their quotas, new states emerge etc. It is intended that future allocations of quotas be determined within the forum of the Open Skies Consultative Commission (OSCC). Numbers of overflights are to be fixed a year in advance, the scheduling for the quarter to be agreed at least six weeks ahead.[58] Such inflexibility could be a significant flaw if the maximum notice provisions are insisted upon by participating states.

Before an overflight can take place 72 hours prior notification must be given of arrival. Once the inspecting aircraft arrives at a specified Point of Entry (POE) it must submit a flight plan 24 hours in advance of the flight.[59] In the interim all the aircraft's sensors are checked. The only restrictions that can be placed on the route of the inspecting aircraft are those made to comply with flight safety restrictions and problems generated by local weather conditions. The Treaty is very specific on the categories of sensors that can be used and the limits of their performance for Open Skies flights.[60] These sensors fall into 4 categories:

- Optical panoramic and framing cameras.
- Video cameras with real time display.
- Infra-red line scanning devices.
- Sideways looking synthetic aperture radar (SAR).

All of this equipment, which must be commercially available to signatories, is of limited technical specification, well below that which is widely available to military purchasers of such equipment.[61] After the flight the sensor data is processed, it then has to be made available to any other state party that requests a copy of it.[62] Data from any flight can be purchased from the observing state by any other signatory and depending on how this is done, i.e. can purchasers select almost individual frames from images covering areas in which they are interested or do they have to buy imagery from the whole flight, costs can be reduced to just a few hundred pounds.[63] Not only is the collection of information a specialised affair but so also is its detailed interpretation and analysis. This sort of specialist analysis tends only to be readily available to the larger military powers in Europe and North America, who already have significant reconnaissance capabilities.

The question of the delay between announcing an Open Skies flight, the aircraft arriving in the country to be inspected and the actual flight being undertaken, provides in excess of 72 hours for concealment in sensitive areas to be undertaken and was an area of importance to the United States in the negotiations. This was the only one of the major conventional agreements that directly affected the territory of the United States. The US has gone to considerable trouble to ensure that this advance notification period can be utilised to undertake concealment. It has developed an automated system known as the 'Passive Overflight Module' (POM) and 'Telephone Notification System' (TNS). Using this the US Defence Threat Reduction Agency, once it has a copy of the agreed flight plan can then notify any registered agency, contractor or military unit affected that it is likely to be overflown together with an indication of the probable sensor coverage that will affect it, using an automated dialing system to provide the warning.[64] The fear that an Open Skies flight might detect field weapon testing, other development or evaluation activities, or information about defence plants and contractors are sufficient that the US is determined to minimise 'information loss'.[65] This has resulted in the development of a special Department of Defence programme known as DTIRP (Defence Treaty Inspection Readiness Programme) to manage the loss of non-treaty information - in effect the old fear that arms control treaties, will enable 'espionage' to take place.[66] Whilst programmes such as this are perfectly permissible, they do something to undermine one of Open Skies greatest benefits, transparency, by encouraging routine concealment.

Participants. Signatories to the Treaty signed on 24th March 1992 were: Belarus, Belgium, Bulgaria, Canada, the Czech Republic, Denmark, France, Georgia, Germany, Greece, Hungary, Iceland, Italy, Kyrgyzstan, Luxembourg, Netherlands, Norway, Poland, Portugal, Romania, Russian Federation, Slovak Republic, Spain, Turkey, Ukraine, UK and the United States. Provisions have also been made for the accession of other OSCE states once the Treaty has been fully ratified.

Full ratification of the agreement has proved a major problem and is still to be completed. The Treaty cannot fully enter into force until 20 states have ratified it, including all of those who have a passive quota of more than eight flights per year therefore, before the Treaty can enter into force Russia and Belarus must complete ratification.[67] Whilst the Treaty is not yet in full operation 'trial overflights' have grown in pace over the last few years. Since 1992 a number of countries have converted a number of aircraft for the purpose of conducting overflights and as these have become available bilateral and multilateral test and trial flights have been conducted. These have included the US, Russia, the UK, Germany, Hungary, Canada, Ukraine, Benelux states, Romania, Czechs and Slovaks, to name just a few. The trial flights appear useful in their own right allowing aircrews, ground crews and observers to become familiar with operating procedures and flight procedures. The difference between 'trial' and 'real' flights is in effect minimal. Those involved have said that the process just of working together to plan flights has acted to build confidence itself and that probably 95% of what could be gained from a live flight can also be achieved from a trial flight.[68] Such tests have also permitted the gradual resolution of a number of technical questions within the

OSCC by providing specimen images from which the working groups could agree solutions and procedures.[69] The trials have also been useful for aircraft certification purposes.

Geographical Area. The treaty applies to the airspace of all signatory states, there is no provision for airspace to be declared 'off limits' other than for immediate flight safety reasons.

Open Skies Consultative Commission

The Open Skies Consultative Commission was an institutional product of the Treaty. It was scheduled to meet at least four times a year with each session lasting a maximum of four weeks. The OSCC is designed to be the forum responsible for dealing with all issues under the Treaty, quota allocation, resolving technical problems, dealing with disputes, accession of new states and general treaty implementation arrangements. Decisions within the OSCC must be made on a consensual basis and the proceedings of the OSCC are confidential unless agreed otherwise.[70] The OSCC first met on April 2nd 1992, only eight days after the Treaty's signature and since that time progress has lacked the previous sense of urgency that the Treaty negotiations had.[71]

In the initial OSCC sessions the neutral OSCE states attended as observers but Turkey resisted any attempts for their position to be strengthened. There was agreement to establish four Working Groups to resolve outstanding issues on cost, sensor calibration, notification procedures and formats and rules of procedure for the OSCC.[72] The issue of cost allocation, mainly disputes between the Americans and Soviets, that was so difficult to resolve in the actual Treaty negotiations that it persisted in the OSCC for over a year before agreement could be reached on who would pay for the operating costs of a flight if the host nation insisted that its own aircraft were used. Equally sensor calibration proved difficult because the Americans use different approaches to the problem, but the Russian military were also said to be trying to use this dispute to reduce the overall intrusiveness of the agreement.[73] The Information Format Working Group had more success trying to harmonise the exchange of information and presentation formats with those of the CFE Treaty and Vienna Documents as far as possible, doing so in 35 out of 37 cases.[74]

In terms of rules of procedure, it was agreed that states which had possessed observer status at the Open Skies conference could also adopt this status during the 1992 OSCC sessions pending some final agreement, which eventually specified the continuance of this procedure until the Treaty fully entered into force.[75] The terms of cost distribution to the operation of the OSCC was particularly important to newly emerged and former WTO intent on preserving their foreign currency holdings.[76] Peter Jones suggests that many of the problems dealt with in the OSCC during 1992 were of a political nature, though often masquerading as technical issues which accounts for much of the time taken to resolve them.[77] Most of the issues outlined above were not formally resolved until the final, plenary, OSCC meeting in July 1993.[78]

Since 1993 progress has continued to be slow. Meetings were held weekly but continue to lack any urgency, perceived to be because of the lack of progress in ratification. As a result meetings were changed to a monthly basis for 1994. A Canadian suggestion that the Treaty provisionally enter into force, as CFE did, was rejected.[79] At OSCC meetings on 18th April and 12th October 1994, a number of technical decisions were taken on calculation of minimum flight altitudes, use of video and line scanning cameras, calibration etc., that were important steps in fleshing out the agreements main terms.[80] Since then OSCC meetings frequencies have declined still further with only three scheduled meetings whilst the Working Groups did not meet at all, as the matters for resolution have now largely been met. The 'test flights' have continued but Russian and Ukranian ratification is appears the only significant problem now.

Expertise and the Vienna Process

Discussion with one official on the operations of the OSCC well illustrates the place of experts in the Vienna arms control process and their relationship to national capitals. Plenary sessions tend to be the place where national statements, which are often the most controversial, are made. State representatives are expected to posture on particular occasions as they are working on the instructions of national capitals. However, it is in the margins where much is achieved. 'About 20% is achieved in formal negotiations and about 80% in informal discussions'.[81] The Plenary sessions are often the places where statements that have very little to do with the work in hand - such as Russian concern about NATO expansion - are made which tend to hinder rather than help work. In private it is the close personal relationships between individuals, either because they have been working together on the same agreements for sometime or because they have had contact with each other in previous postings or jobs, that makes the difference. Over meals or side meetings individuals are able to put aside the posturing and discuss some of the limits or possibility for negotiation and compromise aided by their previous experience with each other or other members of the same delegation. Those working on agreements try to resolve problems at the lowest level, it is only where this is not possible that they tend to be referred back to seniors who then try to deal with the problem and will refer it upwards again if they are unable to clear any difficult point.[82] This is an approach familiar in all diplomatic negotiation processes.

In OSCC Working Groups the atmosphere and interaction can be rather different to that of the plenary sessions. In the case of the Sensor Guidance Document Working Group, referred to earlier this rather large group of nearly 60 people, met periodically but involved individuals travelling from national capitals at the same time augmenting local representatives normally in Vienna. Thus it would involve, in the case of the UK, a scientific and military representative travelling to Group meetings in Vienna to supplement the RAF Squadron Leader who is the UK's resident Vienna 'expert' on the subject. Other states adopted similar approaches too. In this case much of the issues that were being dealt with were scientific and technical (such as techniques for sensor imagery degradation) and the view was expressed that the presence of national defence ministry officials was necessary to give 'political direction' to discussions to ensure agreement was reached as quickly as practicable. Thus visits from national capitals to Vienna present opportunities for networking between those individuals involved in the agreement from national defence and Foreign affairs ministries, local Vienna OSCC and diplomatic experts and some from national verification agencies too. Such networking has also meant that the arrangement of trial flights, at this stage, can be facilitated through opposite number contacts with representatives from other states having similar responsibilities. Thus confidence building was described as a process that can 'percolate upwards' over a period of time as those involved move onto other, and often more senior, jobs.[83]

National Verification Units

Signature of the CFE Treaty, Vienna Documents and later the Treaty on Open Skies generated considerable inspection and hosting commitments sufficient in most instances to require the establishment or expansion of dedicated national military or military-civil units to manage these arrangements. Thus Canada has its Arms Control and Disarmament Division within the Department of External

Affairs; Hungary its Arms Control and Verification Centre (ACVC), the USA has its Defence Threat Reduction Agency (DTRA); the UK's Joint Arms Control Implementation Group (JACIG); French Unite Franciase de Verification (UFV) and the German Zentrum fur Verification der Bundeswehr (ZVBW) to name just some of the largest. Proposals to form a NATO pool of verification experts were soon blocked by France insisting on agreement verification being a national responsibility rather than an Alliance one. An idea to create a CSCE verification centre was still born.[84]

The co-operation and cross training undertaken between these units both within the NATO structure and bi-laterally has been considerable. Published accounts of the experience of the UKs Joint Arms Control Implementation Group (JACIG) demonstrate this. Originally known as the ACG (Arms Control Group) the unit was established within the British Ministry of Defence to support commitments under the CDE process with costs running in the region of £80,000 to host commitments from the Vienna Document (1991 prices) and £20,000 to make such inspections.[85] By 1989 it was clear that future commitments would increase considerably and the decision to create JACIG with a strength of 124 personnel was taken.[86] Cross training in 1991 involved JACIG hosting training inspections by teams from Germany, Belgium, Netherlands, Spain, Hungary, Czechoslovakia, Poland, Soviet Union, Canada and the USA and undertaking personnel exchanges with their German, French, Hungarian and Czechoslovak counterparts.[87]

In 1992 JACIG developed the process further with training activities extended to include co-operation with Finnish, Swedish, Bulgarian, Norwegian, Italian, Polish and Azerbaijani teams.[88] This was in addition to the inspections carried out under Phase 1 of the CFE Treaty (the Baseline Validation Period) and the Vienna Document. At the end of the validation Period 27 of the 30 commandants of Treaty signatories verification units held a joint conference at Royal Air Force Scampton in the United Kingdom to discuss and evaluate their experiences, the major outcome of which appeared to be a strong desire to form mixed nationality inspection teams.[89]

The verification organisations of some other states are analogous to the British. The French re-opened Creil air base near Paris to establish a verification centre with a staff of over 120, in addition to efforts in support of arms control agreements.[90] The German ZVBW employs more than 500 people across 2 sites (100 at the former GDR verification centre at Strausberg near Berlin) to oversee the conduct and hosting of verification visits within the Federal Republic. The creation of the Defence Threat Reduction Agency (via an incarnation as the On-Site Inspection Agency) in the United States resulted from the INF Treaty employs over 850 staff, and undertakes similar activities to other allied agencies but also supports agreements affecting nuclear as well as conventional forces. It is based in Washington DC but also has offices in Japan, Germany, Moscow and Votkinsk in Russia.

For former WTO states the difficulties have been considerably greater. In FSU states responsibility for CFE implementation was quickly passed to foreign and defence ministries. Within the Russian Ministry of Defence the Directorate for Implementing the Reduction of the Armed Forces and Strategic Weapons was created to supervise arrangements. Generally former Soviet states other than Russia, have suffered from a lack of expertise and experienced staff who have traditionally been based in Moscow. There were fears that the cost of destruction might make some states hesitate in complying fully with the destruction obligations. Other WTO members have tended to turn towards the West to seek technical support and assistance.

Conclusions

As we have seen the early 1990s saw a host of agreements come together to regulate affairs in the field of conventional weapons in Europe. In the end they were negotiated quickly - and sometimes incomplete as in the case of the CFE Treaty in particular - all in some ways less than adequate to cope with the post Cold War structural changes and the Soviet Union's demise.

On the one hand we have a reduction in superpower conflict that potentially reduces the significance of the agreements. On the other we have the probability of a less stable Europe - at least towards its currently defined Eastern and Southern fringes - that makes them potentially powerful tools to aid regional stabilisation.

We have some measures such as in the Vienna Documents and Treaty on Open Skies that contribute to the wider stability and are 'all weather' measures. The CFE Treaty is much more specific, attempting to address some detailed categories of equipment, their numbers and deployment, which are thought to be most detrimental to military stability in the region. But it has been unable to fully cope with the reality of political and military change and has as a result been in a continual state of unofficial re-negotiation. Yet even combined these measures have been unable to prevent interstate conflict and increasing intra-state warfare is becoming a more important issue that ought to be tackled. Between them the various measures contain duplications of effort, gaps in coverage and inadequate implementation measures in some situations - there is no synergetic relationship between them. But perhaps most important of all there is no clear way forward for future measures and the reliance on the state as the 'unit of analysis' can make it more difficult to achieve greater levels of interstate cooperation and integration. Reversing both trends ought to be important objectives.

Notes

1   A full Treaty text is contained in: *SIPRI Yearbook 1991: World Armament and Disarmament*, SIPRI, (Oxford University Press: Oxford:), Appendix 13A, pp. 461-88.

2   S. Koulik & R. Kokoski, (1994), *Conventional Arms Control: Perspectives on Verification*, SIPRI, (Oxford University Press: Oxford), p. 19.

3   J. Sharp, (1991), 'Conventional Arms Control in Europe', *SIPRI Yearbook 1991: World Armament and Disarmament*, SIPRI, (Oxford University Press: Oxford), pp. 409-10.

4   Ibid. p. 410.

5   S. Croft, (1994), 'Negotiations, Treaty Terms and Implications', *The Conventional Armed Forces in Europe Treaty: The Cold War Endgame*, S. Croft (ed), (Dartmouth Publishing: Aldershot), p. 31.

6   Koulik & Kokoski, 1994, op. cit. p. 75.

7   R.A. Falkenrath, (1995), *Shaping Europe's Military Order: The Origins and Consequences of the CFE Treaty*, CSIA Studies in International Security, (London: MIT Press), pp. 113-4.

8   Ibid. pp. 245-6.

9   Sharp, (1992a), 'The CFE Treaty and the Dissolution of the Union of Soviet Socialist Republics', in *Verification 1992: Peacekeeping, arms control and the environment*, J. Poole & R Guthrie (eds), (VERTIC: London), p. 25.

10   Sharp, 1991, op. cit. p. 428.

11   Koulik & Kokoski, 1994, op. cit. p. 66.

12   Sharp, 1991, op. cit. p. 428.

13   J. Sharp, (1993), 'Conventional Arms Control in Europe', *SIPRI Yearbook 1993: World Armament and Disarmament*, SIPRI, (Oxford University Press: Oxford), p. 593.

14   Arms Control Reporter, (1992), sheet 407, B485.

15   J. Sharp, (1994), 'Will the CFE Treaty Survive the Cold War?', in *Verification 1994: Peacekeeping, arms control and the environment*, J. Poole & R Guthrie (eds), (Brasseys/VERTIC: London), pp. 162.

16   J. Sharp, (1992), 'Conventional Arms Control in Europe: developments and prospects in 1991', *SIPRI Yearbook 1992: World Armament and Disarmament*, SIPRI, (Oxford University Press: Oxford), p. 613.

17   Sharp, (1994), op. cit. p. 162.

18   Z. Lachowski, (1994), 'The Vienna confidence -and security-building measures', Appendix 14A, *SIPRI Yearbook 1994*, SIPRI, (Oxford University Press: Oxford), p. 568.

19   Falkenrath, (1995), op. cit. p. 231.

20   Falkenrath, (1995), op. cit. p. 232.

21   Sharp, (1993), op. cit. pp. 130-31.

22   Falkenrath, (1995), op. cit. p. 233.

23   Falkenrath, (1995), op. cit. p. 235.

24   Based on IISS calculations, detailed in Table 7.5, Falkenrath, (1995), op. cit. p. 288.

25   Koulik & Kokoski, (1995), op. cit. p. 120.

26   Z. Lachowski, (1994), op. cit. p. 573, R. Falkenrath, (1995), op. cit. p. 236.

27   J.P. Harahan and J.C. Kuhn, (1996), *On-Site Inspections under the CFE Treaty*, (Washington DC: On-Site Inspection Agency), pp. 331-39.

28   Details of the Adaption Process are given in Chapter 6.

29   J. Sharp, (1988), 'Conventional arms control in Europe: problems and prospects', Stockholm International Peace Research Institute, *SIPRI Yearbook 1989: World Armaments and Disarmament*, (Oxford: Oxford University Press), p. 323 and T. Wirth, (1989), 'Confidence and Security Building Measures', in R. Blackwill and S. Larrabee (eds), *Conventional Arms Control and East-West Security*, (Clarendon Press: Oxford), p. 343.

30   J. Borawski, (1991), 'Stability through Openness: the Vienna Negotiations on Confidence and Security Building Measures in Europe', in J. Poole (ed), *Verification Report 1991*, (Apex Press: New York), p. 68.

31   Annex 1, *Vienna Document*, 1994.

32   A. Bloed, (ed), (1993), *The Conference on Security and Co-operation in Europe: Analysis and Basic Documents, 1972-1993*, (Dordrecht: Kluwer Academic), p. 529.

33   J. Sharp, (1991), op. cit. p. 455. Though it was not until 1994 that 32 states were reported as being connected to the system, a significant leap from the 20 of the previous year after technical assistance and training was provided by the UK and USA.

34   HMSO, (1991), *Charter of Paris for A New Europe*, (HMSO: London), Cm. 1464, p. 16.

35   S. Koulik & R. Kokoski, (1994), op. cit. p. 150.

36   Z. Lachowski, (1993), 'The Vienna confidence -and security-building measures in 1992', Appendix 12A, *SIPRI Yearbook 1993*, SIPRI, (Oxford University Press: Oxford), p. 618.

37   J. Borawski, (1993), 'From Helsinki to Vienna and Back', in J. Pooole & R. Guthrie (eds), *Verification Report 1993*, (Brasseys: London), p. 200.
38   S. Koulik and R. Kokoski, 1994, op. cit. p. 151.
39   J. Borawski, (1993), op. cit. p. 200.
40   S. Koulik & R. Kokoski, 1994, op. cit. p. 153.
41   *Vienna Document 1992*, Article VIII, paras 113-15.
42   Ibid. Article III, para. 21.
43   Ibid. Article III, para. 34.
44   C. Hain-Cole, (1995), *Seminar on the OSCE Experience in the Field of Confidence-Building*, Cairo, 26-8th September, 1995.
45   Ibid. Article VIII, paras. 78-90.
46   Z. Lachowski, (1992), 'Implementation of the Vienna Document 1990 in 1991', in *SIPRI Yearbook 1992*, (Oxford: Oxford University Press), p. 492.
47   Z. Lachowski, (1993), op. cit. p. 628.
48   Z. Lachowski, (1994), op. cit. p. 595.
49   *FSC Journals* Nos. 63, 65, 66
50   *FSC Journal* No. 60.
51   *FSC Journal* No. 70 - Annex.
52   OSCE Secretary General, (1995), *Annual Report 1995: On OSCE Activities*, (OSCE: Vienna), p. 33.
53   *FSC./128/97, FSC.AIAM/41/98, FSC.AIAM/41/99*
54   Z. Lachowski, (1994), op. cit. pp. 628-9
55   F. Schimmelfennig, (1993), *Arms Control and the Dissolution of the Soviet Union: Regime Robustness and International Socialization*, Tubinger Arbeitspapiere Zur Internationalen Politik Und Friedensforschung, Nr 21, p. 29.
56   W. Hoynck, (7th March 1994), *CSCE Capabilities for contributing to conflict prevention and crisis management*, p. 3.
57   HMSO, (1992), *Treaty On Open Skies*, Cmnd. No. 2067, pp. 6-8.
58   Ibid. Annex H, Para 3.
59   S. Koulik and R. Kokoski, 1994, op. cit. p. 185.
60   *Treaty on Open Skies*, op. cit. Article IV, Para 1 .
61   Ibid Article IV, Para 2. Also during the interim period of application only the most basic of these sensors can be used unless by prior agreement.
62   Ibid Article IX, Section IV.
63   Again Poland has tested this option in work with the UK sending officers to the UK to look at flight imagery and select particular shots of interest which were then taken to Poland for analysis by national experts. Private Communication, UK MoD Official, September 1996.
64   US, OSIA, (1995), Fact Sheet, *Passive Overllight Module (POM) and Telephone Notification System (TNS)*, (OSIA, May 1995).

65   US, OSIA, (1996), *Facility Overflights under the Open Skies Treaty*, DTIRP Security Information Bulletin No. 3.

66   US OSIA, (1995), *Defence Treaty Inspection Readiness Programme*, (OSIA: Fact Sheet).

67   Foreign & Commonwealth Office, (1996), *Arms Control and Disarmament Review*, No. 40, (Nov 1995-Feb 1996), p. 103.

68   Private discussion UK, MoD official, September 1996.

69   S. Bailer, (1995), 'The Treaty on Open Skies', *SIPRI Yearbook 1995*, SIPRI, (Oxford University Press: Oxford), p. 823.

70   *Treaty on Open Skies* op. cit. Article X and Annex L.

71   *Arms Control Reporter*, (1993), Box 409.

72   P. Jones, 1992, (1992), 'Open Skies: A New Era of Transparency', *Arms Control Today*, May 1992, p. 15.

73   Ibid. p. 157.

74   R. Kokoski, (1993), 'The Treaty on Open Skies', in *SIPRI Yearbook 1993*, SIPRI, (Oxford University Press: Oxford), p. 633.

75   P. Jones, (1992), op. cit. p. 158.

76   Ibid p. 158.

77   Ibid p. 159.

78   Personal Communication, Security Policy Department, Foreign & Commonwealth Office, 19th July 1993.

79   Z. Lachowski, (1994), 'The Treaty on Open Skies', *SIPRI Yearbook 1994*, SIPRI, (Oxford University Press: Oxford), p. 602.

80   S. Bailer, (1995), op. cit. p .823.

81   This supports the survey data in K. Wright, (1998), *European Conventional Arms Control and Epistemic Communities*, PhD thesis, (University of Essex).

82   Discussion with British officials 1996.

83   Discussion, UK MoD Official, September 1996.

84   J. Sharp, (1990), *SIPRI Yearbook 1990: World Armament and Disarmament*, SIPRI, (Oxford University Press: Oxford), p. 160.

85   P. Lewis and P. Zimmerman (1991), ' Costs of Verification', in *Verification 1991: Peacekeeping, arms control and the environment*, J. Poole & R Guthrie (eds), (VERTIC/Apex Press: NY), p. 207.

86   R. Giles, (1992), 'Implementing Arms Control: a Survey of the Work of JACIG', in *Verification 1992: Peacekeeping, arms control and the environment*, J. Poole and R Guthrie (eds), (VERTIC: London), p. 160.

87   Ibid pp. 161-62.

88   For full details see: R. Giles, (1993), 'JACIG sans Frontieres', in *Verification 1993: Peacekeeping, arms control and the environment*, J. Poole and R Guthrie (eds), (Brasseys; VERTIC: London), p. 140.

89   Ibid pp. 141-42.

90   S. Koulik and R. Kokoski, (1994), op. cit. p. 59.

4 The Organisation for Security and Co-operation: Innovation and Limitation

Though the CFE Treaty, Vienna Documents and Treaty on Open Skies were completed in the margins of the CSCE process they were not a formalised part of it. The reaching of the three separate agreements left it with little sense of direction for the development of further measures. Allied to this was the fact the CFE Treaty and the Treaty on Open Skies did not enjoy complete CSCE participation but had only a restricted membership. Though at the time effort was overwhelmingly concentrated on implementation of those agreements - and each had their own arbitration and settlement mechanisms - it was clear that a way forward was needed.

This chapter traces the developments that took place within the context of the C/OSCE during the 1990s. The measures agreed during 1999 - the Adapted CFE Treaty and the 1999 Vienna Document are discussed exclusively in chapter 6.

Origins of the FSC

In the early 1990s the CSCE underwent a major period of institutionalisation which saw it transformed from its more ad-hoc and temporary appearance of the past and eventually led to its transformation into an 'organisation'. However the institutionalisation process was not been a carefully controlled one, or totally successful, as it has shown tendencies for duplication and overlap. Together with weak decision-making powers and under-resourcing, the environment for institutional competition exists within the OSCE, despite attempts to rationalize it.

The 1992 Helsinki Document, along with changes to the overall organisation of CSCE institutions created the Forum for Security Co-operation (and a strengthened CPC).[1] The FSC was to comprise a 'Special Committee' and the Consultative Committee of the Conflict Prevention Centre (CPC). This was initially poorly staffed with only a Director, two staff and some administrative support.[2] To expect the CPC to co-ordinate the 53 delegations concerns and interests, was clearly an unrealistic expectation. Its role became to facilitate the handling of the 'unusual military activities' and 'hazardous military incident' provisions of the 1990 agreement. In terms of a division of labour within the CSCE it was intended that the FSC deal more with 'military' matters whilst the Committee of Senior Officials (now the Permanent Council) concentrated on 'political' issues; although it was generally recognized that any such division of work was not so easily effected. The FSC was linked to the Conflict Prevention Centre by the fact that the CPC's Special Committee is composed of the same delegations that comprise the FSC to ensure continuity.[3] It was the Special Committee that undertook the Annual Implementation Assessment Meetings (AIAM) required by the 1992 Vienna Document.[4] When the Consultative Committee was dissolved and the Permanent Committee (now Permanent Council) created at the 1993 Rome Council meeting, activities relating to arms control and military aspects of security were transferred to the FSC, with the exception of the competence for convening meetings under the mechanisms of unusual military activities, which was assumed by the Permanent Committee. The Special Committee was renamed the FSC on 11 January 1995 finally rationalizing the overly complex organisational structure.

Even thought the organisational structure was complex the FSC was given an extremely wide mandate with a formidable agenda under two broad headings; that of arms control, disarmament, confidence and security building; and secondly, security enhancement and cooperation.[5] The aim of the FSC was:

> to start a new negotiation on arms control, disarmament, confidence and security-building, to enhance regular consultation and to intensify co-operation among them on matters related to security and to further the process of reducing the risk of conflict.[6]

This agenda was given initial form with a Programme for Immediate Action (PIA) part of which was intended to improve information exchange, harmonization, and further developments of the Vienna Document.[7]

The FSC has met almost weekly since its inception, in Vienna's Neuer Saal, though progress has been slow and the Forum is generally perceived as performing well below its potential.[8] Its work was divided between two Working Groups A and B (WGA and WGB). WGA dealt largely with issues contained in an Annex to the Programme for Immediate Action (PIA).[9] WGB covered measures under the heading of 'Security Enhancement and Co-operation', such as defence conversion, and regional issues. Within both general CSCE discussions and the FSC concern has been expressed over the numbers of state actors, the pressures that the requirement for consensus decision making generates and the consequent effect this has on the nature, depth and scope of decisions made. Such concerns suggest that the probability of defection and the difficulties of taking sanctions against non-compliers will create serious problems for meaningful co-operation.[10] It was also reported after the FSCs first round of meetings that great expectations should not be attached to it. Similarly one NATO head of delegation commented that the pressure to achieve results within the FSC was not high because the sort of harmonization issues it had been asked to deal with so far were not high on the agenda of European security concerns.[11] By 1992 it was also becoming increasingly apparent that CSBMs of the Stockholm and Vienna type were regarded as markedly less important, and increasingly overshadowed by other interests, than they were previously.[12]

Despite the apparent urgency attached to the PIA progress was slow and Decisions in a number of areas on the 'Global Exchange of Military Information', a 'Code of Conduct on Politico-Military Aspects of Security' and 'Principles Governing Conventional Arms Transfers' were only agreed on the eve of the OSCE's Budapest Summit, after a marathon 3 day session. A fortnight previously the texts were still awaiting presentation to national capitals for approval.[13] The agreed texts were included in the 1994 Vienna Document at the Budapest OSCE Summit which incorporated all the measures in previous Vienna Document's. The proposals on conventional arms transfers agreed at Budapest were so thin that it was largely left to an FSC Seminar in June 1995, operating through a number of Working Groups, to provide some conclusions to give a more concrete form to the Budapest Declaration.[14] Regional arms control measures were given some attention in 3 day Seminar in Vienna during July 1995 and WGA was asked to pursue the subject bi-weekly in October to December 1995.[15]

Norm & Standard Setting Measures

There has also been a marked change in the type of measures under negotiation. Whereas in the past measures had a tangible element be it in terms of information provision or face to face contact and thus were all verifiable to a greater or lesser extent. These new forms of measures known as Norm & Standard Setting Measures represent something very different from the style of measures in the Vienna Documents. They are much more clearly addressed to the political level, orientated to reinforcing states commitments to principles or action already agreed to in other international treaties or extending them further. However, their very nature makes them much more difficult to verify and rely almost exclusively on action at the diplomatic and political level to ensure compliance. The terms of the measures makes their success much more difficult to assess.

The main agreements under this heading are:

Principles Governing Non-proliferation - which relates to weapons of mass destruction and missile technology referring almost entirely to the Non Proliferation Treaty, Missile Technology Control Regime, IAEA standards and the Biological Weapons Convention.

Code of Conduct on Politico-Military Aspects of Security.[16] Talks largely of how signatories are free to organise their own security arrangements, how military and internal security personnel should be trained and operate within the accords of national and international law in respect to human rights. Participants at the 1997 and 1999 Follow-up conferences stressed Code's value was as an instrument contributing to the democratic control of the armed forces - especially so for some of the Central and East European states.[17]

Global Exchange of Military Information (GEMI). Of this series of agreements the GEMI is probably the most detailed. It requires states to provide information on the holdings of whole range of military forces and equipment held by member states, going well beyond the requirements of the Vienna Documents, though at a fairly generalised level. GEMI has created problems in that to a certain extent it overlaps with some of the information contained in Vienna Document Information Exchange, but its timetable for delivery is different creating a certain amount of duplication. The supply of information of GEMI from many states is often late and some participants are keen to try and simplify the process perhaps merging the two.

Stabilizing Measures for Localised Crisis Situations. This document provides a non-exhaustive menu of specific measures that could be applied in crisis situations assuming armed conflict had not broken out or a cease fire was in place. This extensive 'catalogue' builds on sections contained in the 1992

Vienna Document and includes talks about transparency measures, extraordinary information exchange, the notification of certain military activities, notification of plans for acquisition and deployment of major weapon and equipment systems, measures of constraint, the introduction and support of a cease-fire, the establishment of demilitarized zones, cessation of military flights, the deactivation of certain weapon systems, the treatment of irregular forces, constraints on certain military activities, measures to reinforce confidence, public statements on matters relevant to a particular crisis situation, the observation of certain military activities, setting up of liaison teams, establishment of direct lines of communication, joint expert teams in support of crisis management, joint co-ordination commissions or teams. It also lists a number of measures that could be used to monitor compliance and evaluate outcomes - examination of data provided under any extraordinary information exchange, inspections, observing compliance with demilitarized zones, verification locations of heavy weapons, challenge inspections and the introduction of an aerial observation regime.[18]

A number of other measures have also been implemented under the Programme for Immediate Action Series, including measures on *Defence Planning*, that attempt to provide greater transparency and information exchange at the political level of force, equipment and operation planning and budgeting over a five year perspective in some instances. This has been another measure that has been cited as a valuable tool for some of the transition states to implement their own programmes to ensure democratic control of their armed forces.

The Programme of Military Contacts and Co-operation outlines exchange and contact and joint training/exercise programmes that might be made between the air, naval and land forces of participating states.[19] Indeed this has been a very weak area of activity - much of it now being superceded by the activities taking place under NATO's Partnership for Peace Programme. The *Principles Governing Conventional Arms Transfers* requires another information exchange that essentially duplicates the requirements for states to annually provide information to the United Nations Register of Conventional Arms - even providing the information in the same format.[20]

Vienna as the Centre of an Epistemic Arms Control Community

Vienna is one of the primary locations for expertise in European conventional arms control and confidence building activity, having been central to the whole process for in excess of twenty five years. The potential size of the Vienna arms control 'community' can be estimated as being relatively small probably numbering around 90-100 people +/- 10%.[21] In addition to Ambassadors and/or Heads of Delegation being involved in the chairing of meetings and co-ordinating efforts, even medium size states such as Germany and the UK tend now to have a maximum of 4 or 5 individuals even peripherally engaged upon arms control work. Of course with smaller states their whole delegation may only number 1 or 2 people in total. Arms control related work is also only one in a wide range of activities that have to be covered by national delegations to the OSCE. Georgia and Iceland do not maintain delegations in Vienna at all. In other cases the delegations themselves feel that they have no expertise present in arms control and so rarely take part in any of these activities. Other states including: San Marino, Liechtenstein and The Holy See - in addition to Iceland, maintain no registered armed forces and so their participation in security activities is likely to be low anyway.

However, it is often difficult to determine precisely who is engaged on arms control work in Vienna at any one time. Conversations indicate that although Ambassadors often chair and participate in FSC and other meetings, they tend to regard themselves largely as facilitators rather than as part of the arms control 'community' themselves. Although Ambassadors have a part to play they tend to regard arms control and confidence-building as an area of 'specialist expertise'. This expertise is largely drawn from a mixture of diplomatic and military staff. These individuals share a variety of characteristics. Few stay in Vienna more than 4 years, being rotated periodically, largely according to the regulations and needs of their own services. Most are involved in ongoing work with both their own and other delegations in Vienna. Significant proportions are also involved in liaison and consultation work with staff in national capitals. As the basis of delegations in Vienna is a state one then such affiliation must be a defining factor. Some of the individuals have been, are or are likely to be involved in arms control related work for sometime.[22]

One notable point is the general absence in Vienna of technical experts that are associated with arms control verification which tends to be 'imported' for relatively short periods and specific tasks. What is also clear is that most of the expertise is located in national defence ministries but more especially national verification units. Thus whilst technical expertise might rest with 'imported' experts they are as much policy 'advisers' as they are 'decision-makers'. Their advice is policy relevant but not the single most important determinant, though it can inform national interest determination. Similarly we see no evidence that as, Adler claims for the nuclear arms control community, that technical experts were able to use their expertise to gain 'political legitimation and authority',[23] rather they were just one part of the overall decision-making mechanism.

Trying to Reinvigorate the Process

One constant concern for the OSCE has been measures that have a standardised application throughout the OSCE. There has always been the fear that measures adopted for specific situations may not be appropriate for other future disputes, so that attaching the OSCE label to a specific set of measures them would set 'dangerous' precedents for the future. The FSC has indicated its desire to develop the NSSM approach in future measures further but again the process has lacked any real sense of urgency mainly because of a lack on interests in many of the participating states.

Whilst progress has been slow the FSC is tasked with taking the whole security process and though there has been a significant preoccupation with the Common Comprehensive Security Model the 1996 OSCE Lisbon Summit produced two significant documents in arms control terms - *The Framework for Arms Control &The Development of the Agenda of the FSC*.

Framework for Arms Control

The Framework explicitly recognised important issues that had been a part of FSC discussions for sometime in two particular areas. First, was the concern that not only interstate but also intra-state conflict can spread to surrounding areas. Second, that regional arms control measures should be considered in certain - though unspecified circumstances - where particular issues arise but that they should not detract from OSCE wide measures.

The section on challenges and risks in the document remain familiar to those of the Cold War period and illustrate the main military concerns of the participating states on the continent:

- military imbalances that may contribute to instabilities;
- inter-State tensions and conflicts, in particular in border areas, that

affect military security;
- internal disputes with the potential to lead to military tensions or conflicts between States;
- enhancing transparency and predictability as regards the military intentions of States;
- helping to ensure democratic political control and guidance of military, paramilitary and security forces by constitutionally established authorities and the rule of law;
- ensuring that the evolution or establishment of multinational military and political organizations is fully compatible with the OSCE is comprehensive and co-operative concept of security, and is also fully consistent with arms control goals and objectives;
- ensuring that no participating State, organization or grouping strengthens its security at the expense of the security of others, or regards any part of the OSCE area as a particular sphere of influence;
- ensuring that the presence of foreign troops on the territory of a participating State is in conformity with international law, the freely expressed consent of the host State, or a relevant decision of the United Nations Security Council;
- ensuring full implementation of arms control agreements at all times, including times of crisis;
- ensuring through a process of regular review undertaken in the spirit of co-operative security, that arms control agreements continue to respond to security needs in the OSCE area;
- ensuring full co-operation, including co-operation in the implementation of existing commitments, in combatting terrorism in all its forms and practices.[24]

The intention of the existing and any new measures agreed being to build a comprehensive 'web' of arms control agreements.

Development of the FSC's Agenda

This document reiterates several elements of the *Framework* on regional measures and the web of the agreements. It also reaffirms the importance of full implementation of the existing agreements, enhancing the existing measures - particularly the NSSM's. Perhaps the most interesting part of the Agenda is its Annex that lists some preliminary ideas advanced by individual member states on particular areas for possible future discussion. These were:

- Extension of CSBMs to naval activities.
- Exchange of information on internal security forces.
- Measures concerning the stationing of armed forces.
- Co-operation in defence conversion.
- Measures concerning the deployment of armed forces on foreign territories, including their trans-border movements.
- Regular seminars on military doctrine (to be held at a high military level).
- An 'OSCE White Paper' on defence issues, based on existing OSCE information.
  regimes and drawing on national experiences.
- Studying the possibility of the creation of zones in Europe free of nuclear weapons.
- Voluntary participation, on a national basis, in verification and information exchange of regional regimes.
- Transparency with regard to structural, qualitative and operational aspects of armed forces.
- Unilateral declaration of weapons ceilings.[25]

Some suggestions, such as the extension of CSBM's to naval activities, are long standing ones, several had relevance to CFE Treaty Review and (cross border force movement) NATO enlargement (force stationing) and existing NSSM's. The proposal to provide an information exchange of internal security forces being perhaps the most far reaching. Whilst both Documents are wide ranging they are vague on the specifics of how objectives might be achieved. Both have been described as 'wish lists' by some participants, with a considerable degree of overlap between them. Few expected that they would provide the necessary new impetus to the wider process.

Common & Comprehensive Security Model (CCSM)

As discussions have slowly progressed on the development of specific measures to aid security and stability in the region the OSCE has also been engaged in a potentially far further reaching exercise in attempting to develop a 'Common and Comprehensive' Security Model for Europe. However, so far arriving at something significant to give substance to the concept has proved extremely difficult. Discussion of what became known as the Common & Comprehensive Security Model began in the early 1990s and gradually gained ground. By 1994 it was becoming a major objective within the OSCE for the participating states but inevitably there were a number of cross cutting forces in place. The Russians at the time were keen on developing the OSCE, at the expense of NATO, as the primary security institution on the continent , where it had equal status with other states and the consensus decision-making principles safeguarded its position. On the other side we have NATO member states in particular were generally attempting to protect the Alliances position and their 'privileged' place within it. But somewhere in between there was the recognition that the old concepts based almost purely on only military elements of security were outdated and that account had to be taken of a much wider and inclusive approach in re-defining the elements of security.

The 1996 OSCE Lisbon Summit was intended to provide the launching pad for the CCSM but the slow, and often contradictory negotiations, made this impossible. There were concerns that the consistency of the OSCE approach be maintained so that other OSCE institutions were not undermined. The Lisbon Declaration itself demonstrates many of the inherent problems that CCSM development faced. There is explicit recognition of the wide range of security threats that Europe faces:

> Human rights are not fully respected in all OSCE States. Ethnic tension, aggressive nationalism, violations of the rights of persons belonging to national minorities, as well as serious difficulties of economic transition, can threaten stability and may also spread to other States. Terrorism, organized crime, drug and arms trafficking, uncontrolled migration and environmental damage are of increasing concern to the entire OSCE community.[26]

The commitment of states to solve these problems was however limited to recognising the provisions of previous agreements, rejection of the use of force, freedom for states to engage (or not) in military alliances. As an examination of the report on the Security Model Discussion during 1995-96 by the then CiO shows consensus, even on the models parameters, were a long way from being reached let alone agreement on any substantive issues.[27] The work on the security model was to continue with an agenda that most interestingly was to cover the definition of a 'Platform for Co-operative Security' to develop 'modalities for cooperation between the OSCE and other security organisations' though little else that was to prove significant.[28] It was clear that though there was recognition of a wider definition of security, the extent of that definition could not be agreed upon between the participating states - often for concern of duplicating, complicating or interfering upon the work of other OSCE institutions and international agreements. But by trying to avoid such complications there was no clear ground upon which to build the model. Under the auspices of the Framework of the CCSM the OSCE explored the 'new' areas of security with a seminar on 'Specific Risks and Challenges' in Vienna during May 1997[29] that looked at drug trafficking, terrorism and organised crime. Whilst another, the 'Seminar on Regional Security and Co-operation' was held the following month but dealt with far more familiar issues. In September another CCSM seminar was held 'Implications for the Mediterranean Basin' on security issues in the area and possible OSCE responses.

The original high hopes for the CCSM have long since disappeared and indeed the measures that have resulted from the many discussions about it have been extremely modest. Meanwhile serious work upon the concept has been discreetly transformed into trying to agree a 'Platform for Co-operative Security' to which participating states can subscribe.[30] That the OSCE has largely been unsuccessful in attempting to create this model does not come as much of a surprise. Not only can the usual reasons for OSCE ineffectiveness be cited - weak decision-making mechanisms and institutions but no other international body has been successful either. There is still the difficulty that exists between building upon a narrow but relatively comprehensible and quantifiable concept, such as military security (with arms control and confidence building representing an even narrower band within that), to a security concept that is much broader, with no clear boundaries and that ultimately could include almost any concern that individuals regard as threatening has therefore proved more difficult to define.

The Dayton Agreement

If developing a comprehensive model of security has proved impossible the basic design of measures contained in the Vienna Documents have proved adaptable to application in post-conflict Bosnia with the General Framework Agreement for Peace in Bosnia and Herzegovina - the Dayton Peace Accords. As a first step part of the agreement related to confidence building measures agreed in January 1996 and later in the year the agreement of a text relating to sub regional arms control. Many of the measures in these agreements were based upon articles originating in the Vienna Documents and CFE Treaty.

Ongoing management of the operation has been undertaken by the Office for Regional Stabilisation as part of the OSCE Mission to Bosnia and Herzegovina.

The Vienna Agreement, January 1996

This agreement was negotiated under the auspices of the OSCE and chaired of Hungarian Ambassador Istvan Gyarmati in early January. A large number of individuals from national OSCE Delegations of the Contact Group states were involved in the negotiation process. A significant number of those involved were military officers having experience with operation of CFE and the Vienna Documents and it was natural that these agreements should serve as the basic model for elaboration.

The Vienna Document provided some 12 measures:
- Exchange of Military information.
- Notification of changes in Command Structure of Equipment Holdings.
- Risk Reduction.
- Notification and Observation of and Constraint on Certain Military activities.
- Restrictions on Military Deployments and Exercises in Certain Geographic Areas.
- Restraints on the Reintroduction of Foreign Forces.
- Withdrawal of Forces and Heavy Weapons to Cantonment/Barracks or Other Designated Areas.
- Restrictions on Locations of Heavy Weapons.
- Notification of Disbandment of Special Operations and Armed Civilian Groups.
- Identification and Monitoring of Weapons Manufacturing Capabilities.
- Programme of Military Contracts and Co-operation.
- Principles Governing Non-Proliferation.

The basic definitions of agreement - such as what constitutes heavy equipment, armed aircraft etc, which had proved problematical during MBFR and CFE talks, were now widely understood and generally accepted. Many of the measures themselves - information exchange, programmes of contact, notification and constraint, risk reduction - are all familiar - but many went further such as ensuring police and para-military formations were included in addition to military units. Similarly, the measure on weapons manufacturing capability identification took the Vienna provisions a stage further. In addition to the measures themselves compliance issues were to be dealt with by the establishment of a Joint Consultative Commission (JCC). Verification was to be established mainly through on-site inspections in accordance with a protocol largely familiar to Vienna Document Observers. In the early stages much of the process was to be overseen by the Personal Representative of the OSCE Chairman in Office. The Programme of Contacts has seen a number of seminars organised for the state parties, for example that on politico-military issues and democratic control (1996), regional confidence building and 'Open Skies' (1997) and Review Meetings in 1998 and 1999. Many of these meetings, though properly attended by the parties, have represented compliance with the agreement rather than actively contributing to a real 'spirit' of confidence building.

Agreement on Sub-Regional Arms Control

The June 1996 agreement on sub regional arms control reached in Florence follows the CFE formula. The agreement covered a wider geographical area applying to the numbers of tanks, armoured combat vehicles, artillery, aircraft and helicopters held by the Republic of Bosnia and Herzegovina, the two Bosnian entities, Croatia and the Federal Republic of Yugoslavia reducing the overall equipment holdings by about 25% of the 1996 figure. Verification was divided into familiar phases commencing with baseline validation and compliance to be discussed within the context of a Sub Regional Consultative Commission (SRCC).

Overall this agreement and that on confidence building have been successfully implemented. The inspection process has been conducted satisfactorily, though on occasions there has been a slight slippage in programmes. The reduction process has been conducted adequately but much of the credit for successful implementation appears to rest with both IFOR and SFOR rather than being due to the parties themselves. Though verification of the agreements rests with the OSCE and the respective parties the role of I/SFOR has been significant. SFOR, for its own purposes gathers information on existing armaments and their deployment, initially at over some 700 locations. It has been estimated that in a standard SFOR brigade one entire company is engaged full-time on arms control activities.[31] SFOR with the military means it has available and that which it can call upon undoubtedly provide a coercive edge to ensure overall compliance with the agreements. Some believe that the absence of involvement from SFOR, or an SFOR like capability, would see the arms control provisions quickly fail. The entity armed forces and those of the Bosnian Federation itself have continued to develop along their own lines rather than developing integrated approaches to training and operations that illustrate the real difficulties that confidence building can face.[32]

The Development of Regional Measures

Developing regional measures of arms control has long been a subject of interest to the OSCE. It had been felt that the pan-European measures of the Vienna Documents were not always best suited to managing more localised tensions that sometimes exist between neighbouring states. There was an expectation that the development of sub-regional measures might be another useful conflict management tool. However, the CCSM Seminar held in Vienna during June 1997 on 'Regional Security and Co-operation' illustrated the serious difficulties this approach faces in practice. The seminar received presentations from sub-regional organisations such as the Barents Euro-Arctic Council, Council of Baltic Sea States, Central European Free Trade Area among others. These highlighted the primarily economic and environmental functions of these bodies but failed to convincingly demonstrate their contribution to security, other than at the very broadest level of 'increasing co-operation'.

A distinction was also made between what were coined 'military' and 'civic' elements of security. The existing Vienna Document and CFE measures were regarded as outdated whilst PfP was highlighted as a measure going beyond because traditional confidence-building. Civic measures received little definitional attention.[33]

The inconclusiveness of the seminar again reflects the immensity of the problems to be solved. On the one hand there is no generally adequate definition of security that reflects anything other than the military aspects on which sub-regional efforts can focus. On the other hand the military threats at sub-regional level are, as often as not, sub-national possibly straddling a number of international borders, that the OSCE approach, rooted as it is on the sovereignty of its member states, is unable to adequately capture. Where sub-regional arms control has taken place in the former Yugoslavia it has been based on coercion of the parties rather than taking place in a spirit of genuine mutual co-operation that is necessary to make it convincing.

Conclusions

This chapter has tried to chart the rather haphazard development of continued conventional arms control and confidence building negotiations from the mid 1990s onwards. In doing so it becomes clear that not only is the institutionalisation of the process complicated but that it has also lacked any firm direction and an element of strong leadership.

That the institutional structure is weak is unsurprising. The existing measures were originally negotiated in the margins of the then CSCE and most importantly between the two military blocs that dominated the continent. In the end the measures concluded were done so rapidly partly for fear of losing agreements altogether. They then remained within the circle of OSCE activity as there was no other suitable location for their institutional creations to be based. As the OSCE went through an unplanned, and uneven, period of instiutionalisation in the 1990s it was unsurprising that military security issues should also be affected by attempts to regularise the organisation of this pan-European body. However, the FSC has generally lacked any real impetus or purpose since its inception except for the conclusion of minor goals. But this as much reflects the general uncertainty of the member states themselves rather than just poor organisation, and difficult decision-making processes, though the OSCE undoubtedly has wider problems in these areas too. States wanted to keep military issues 'under control' but military security issues, increasingly lost the attention of policy makers as they looked towards wider, though ill defined concepts of security, more attractive areas like EU and NATO enlargement. States often looked to how they might best utilise their network of international organisational relationships to better serve state interests.

The attempts to formulate the Common and Comprehensive Security Model illustrate just how difficult such a concept is to operationalise - especially when it might seriously cut across other vested institutional and state interests. Equally it has to be said that even by as early as 1992 there was a real fatigue with the process of military negotiations especially when it looked as if they were likely to become near redundant. The attempts to move into developing Norm and Standard Setting Measures has also proved a difficult leap to make, especially in an atmosphere when there is little interest in further military measures because they are seen as unnecessary, where even achieving full compliance with existing measures has not always proved possible. The implementation of NSSM's is also more difficult as they often require changes in doctrinal approach and attitude which can become true by declaration but can be very difficult to actually verify.

What has proved valuable however is the 'Vienna approach'. The securing of generally agreed definitions on equipment and a number of principal measures and the verification arrangements have provided a valuable vocabulary and menu of measures that can be adopted for use in post-conflict situations as we have seen in Bosnia and Herzegovina through the Dayton accords. But what the Bosnian experience has highlighted is that if the measures are not executed with a truly cooperative spirit, or alternatively with some coercive element to support them they are unlikely to be entirely successful. Even with an element of coercion whilst it might be possible to enforce arms control elements of agreements, confidence building becomes a 'required task' unlikely to really contribute to the building of mutual trust and understanding which such measures were intended to do.

The tasks remain ensuring compliance with existing measures, but also finding a sense of direction, providing leadership, developing more appropriate measures, coping with wider changes in the international security environment and doing so within a more effectively structured institutional framework. These amount to a very tall order indeed.

Notes

1   HMSO, (1992), *CSCE Helsinki Document 1992: The Challenges of Change*, (HMSO: London), Cm 2092, pp. 28-35.

2   I. Peters, (1995), 'CSCE', in E. Kirchner, C. Bluth and J. Sperling (eds), (Dartmouth: Aldershot), p. 71.

3   J Borawski, (1993), 'From Vienna to Helsinki and Back', in J.B. Poole, and R. Guthrie, (1993), *Verification Report 1993: Yearbook on Arms Control, Peacekeeping and the Environment*, (London: Brasseys/VERTIC), p. 203 and HMSO, 1992, Cm 2092 op. cit. p. 30.

4   After dissolution of the Consultative Committee on 8th November 1993.

5   Ibid., pp. 201-203.

6   HMSO, 1992, Cm 2092 op. cit. p. 28.

7   Helsinki Decisions 1992, V.8.

8   A. Rotfeld, (1993), 'The CSCE: Towards a security organisation', *SIPRI Yearbook 1991*, SIPRI, (Oxford University Press: Oxford), pp. 183-4.

9   *FSC Journal No. 4*, essentially development and harmonization of the existing agreements.

10   H. Milner, (1992), 'International Theories of Co-operation Among Nations', *World Politics*, Vol. 44, No. 3, p. 473.

11   J. Borawski, (1993), op. cit. p. 205.

12   Z. Lachowski, (1992), op. cit. p. 618.

13   *FSC Journal No. 91.*

14   *FSC Journal No. 122.*

15   *FSC Journal Nos. 122 & 128.*

16   For a detailed description and analysis of the code see G de Nooy (1996), (ed), *Co-operative Security, the OSCE, and its Code of Conduct*, (Kluwer: the Hague).

17   OSCE, (1997), *Follow -up Conference on the OSCE Code of Conduct on politico-military aspects of security*, Vienna, 22-24 September 1997, FSC.GAL/15/97, pp. 7-8 and OSCE, (1999), *Second Follow -up Conference on the OSCE Code of Conduct on politico-military aspects of security*, Vienna, 29-30 June 1999, FSC.GAL/82/99.

18   *FSC Journal No. 49, Annex 2*

19   *FSC Journal No. 49*

20   *FSC.DEC/13/97*

21   Estimate based upon responses and conversations with a number of Delegation's officials.

22   For survey evidence see K. Wright, (1998), *European Conventional Arms Control and Epistemic Communities*, PhD thesis, (University of Essex).

23   E. Adler, (1992), 'The emergence of cooperation: national epistemic communities and the international evolution of the idea of nuclear arms control', *International Organization*, Vol. 46, No. 1, p. 140.

24   OSCE Lisbon Document, DOC.S/1/96, *Framework for Arms Control*, Para. 7, 3rd December 1996.

25   OSCE Lisbon Document, DOC.S/1/96, *The Development of the Agenda of the FSC*, Annex A, 3rd December 1996.

26   OSCE, (1996), Lisbon Declaration on a Common and Comprehensive Security Model for Europe for the Twenty-First Century, *Lisbon Document*, p. 6.

27   OSCE (1996), *The Security Model Discussion 1995-1996: Report of the Chairman-in-Office to the Lisbon Summit*, REF.S/82/96/Rev.1.

28   Ibid. p. 8.

29   OSCE, (1997), OSCE Security Model Seminar 'Specific Risks and Challenges', REF.PC/362/97, 22nd May 1997.

30   See chapter 6.
31   WEU, (1996), *The role of Europe in Bosnia and Herzegovina*, WEU
        Document 1541, p. 10.
32   WEU, (1999), *Monitoring the Situation in the Balkans*, WEU Document
        1653, pp. 13-14.
33   OSCE, (1997), OSCE Security Model Seminar, '*Regional Security and Co-
        operation*', REF:PC/498/97.

5 NATO and Conventional Arms Control: From Closed Alliance to Real Co-operation

Introduction

The North Atlantic Alliance, as the security focus for most West European states since 1949 has almost inevitably played an important part in the evolution of conventional arms control negotiations. It has done this through two main organs namely the High Level Task Force (HLTF) and its Verification Co-ordination Committee (VCC). The HLTF is primarily a diplomatic negotiating body for Alliance members whilst the VCC and the Verification Implementation Co-ordination Section (VICS) which supports it, have a more 'pragmatic' focus addressing the implementation of verification procedures. At the height of the Cold War NATO provided a negotiating forum for the Allies to decide and coordinate its arms control policy which would then be the position for national CSCE Delegations in Vienna. But the collapse of the Soviet Union has provided it with an opportunity for an enhanced role. It has had to be, in some instances, the prime mover to push the negotiated arrangements forward, it has also been the institution in which training and inspections have been coordinated and as an avenue through which relationships with the former adversary states could be advanced. This gradual process of development provides a basis which suggests that NATO, through its Euro Atlantic Partnership Council, provides a more viable forum for managing the consolidation of existing measures, and possibly developing new ones, than does the present structure with its roots in the OSCE.

Developing Negotiating Positions: NATO and the High Level Task Force

Available information concerning the development of Western negotiating position in the CFE negotiations highlights many of the major and minor, differences between Alliance members. Resolving these differences was a prolonged process for NATO taking it nearly three years from the Budapest

Appeal and NATO's own Ottawa Declaration, later in the Summer of 1986 until just prior to the actual negotiations in March 1989, to formulate an internal negotiating position on CFE.[1] Jennone Walker attributes many of the disagreements that emerged between the NATO members to political, rather than 'security' factors, but especially the suspicions and differences between Washington and Paris over the bloc-to-bloc negotiating approach favoured by the US and the state basis that the French preferred.[2]

The May 1986 Halifax North Atlantic Council meeting created a 'High Level Task Force' in response to Gorbachev's 'Budapest Appeal' of the previous March. Initially the HLTF gave the French in particular serious political problems - even though it had originated from a joint Anglo-French initiative. France was vehemently opposed to inter-bloc negotiations, refusing to accept the principle of intra-alliance ceilings on equipment holdings also seeking a wider linkage to the 35 states of the CSCE[3] that would distance it from the US and give it maximum autonomy within the Alliance.[4] Other early French objections meant nuclear weapon questions were totally excluded, and the talks themselves conducted away from Vienna. On the nuclear issue the French were supported by both the United Kingdom and the United States[5] the latter because of the modernization to SRNF that would soon have to be considered. Additionally the British were themselves suspicious of initiatives that might limit their own nuclear weapons holdings as indeed were the French. In Germany approaching Federal elections saw the CDU/CSU opt against a 'third zero' but wanted parallel negotiations on much lower nuclear ceilings.[6]

Winner and McNerney suggest that the HLTF gave flank states such as Norway, Turkey and Greece a direct say in Alliance arms control policy for the first time.[7] France was vehemently opposed to inter-bloc negotiations, refusing to accept the principle of intra-alliance ceilings on equipment levels.[8] Important internal tasks for the HLTF involved agreeing what categories of weapons ought to be included in the negotiations, how limitations ought to be structured, and probably most important of all, translating NATO's conventional policy goals, aims and objectives into some form of proposals which could be taken to the negotiating table.[9]

The result of French insistence on the HLTF not being directly subordinated to NATO meant that it could not be staffed by permanent national representatives to NATO. Instead, representatives had to report back to their national capitals rather than to the NAC, as had been the case during the MBFR talks.[10] This was a process that inevitably slowed the Alliance's policy formulation. This complication effectively meant that there were 3 levels of negotiation taking place within the Alliance on top of the negotiations themselves.

- Intra-government policy development talks in national capitals.
- Alliance policy formulation in the HLTF based in Brussels.
- 'Caucus consultations' in Vienna to refine and agree a tactical approach within the negotiations.[11]

All of this even before ideas and proposals reached discussion over the negotiating table with the WTO in Vienna. Another level of negotiation ought to be added in that prior to the stages above policy formulation or frameworks had also to be devised within national capitals first. One example of the difficulties this sometimes posed were outlined by Rogers and Williams who stated

> the vagaries of bureaucratic and domestic politics in Washington, in particular, meant that the internal negotiations were sometimes even more time consuming and complex that the negotiations with the adversary.[12]

The HLTF report to NATO in 1986, was embodied in the Brussels Declaration, suggested that the gains of the recently concluded CDE talks in Stockholm be built upon and 2 separate negotiation processes begun:

- The 35 CSCE states to develop further the results of the Stockholm Conference.
- That the states whose relationship had the most direct bearing on military stability in Europe, namely the 23 members of WTO and NATO seek to eliminate disparities and establish conventional stability at lower levels.[13]

Work on resolving intra-alliance differences continued within the HLTF right up to the start of the CFE talks in early 1989. The French participation very much illustrated the improved state of Franco-US relations and the increasing French interest in NATO that had discretely taken place under Mitterrand.[14]

Richard Falkenrath's research disclosed the existence of a small, informal group known as the 'Quint'. This group comprising representatives from the US, UK, Germany, France and Italy, and was originally kept secret from the smaller NATO members. It was used as a forum where differences between its members were resolved, prior to discussion in the HLTF itself.[15] However, the Quint was generally unpopular with smaller HLTF members and did not prevent serious disputes between NATO members surfacing.[16]

Thus the HLTF was a hybrid body, very much of NATO but not directly staffed by it and involving frequent consultation between national capitals and Brussels. Once the CFE Treaty and the Vienna Documents were agreed the profile of the HLTF dipped somewhat but it experienced a resurgence, particularly in preparation for the 1996 CFE Review conference. Whilst HLTF matters are not officially a NATO responsibility the close extent of co-operation between Alliance Headquarters and its members sometimes makes this distinction very small. Whilst HLTF representatives are not drawn from NATO national delegations their deputies frequently are.[17] National delegation activity and participation is said to be affected by a number of factors including their interest in CFE, whether a state has specific views on a particular issue, whilst some states deliberately opt for a 'no position' view until the direction of the argument becomes clear. As much HLTF contact is in written rather than oral form this makes positioning easier.[18]

One deputy representative said he considered personal contacts and the relationships built with other deputies as particularly useful, allowing for co-ordination and the informal exchange of national positions. These relationships were largely built outside of the formal framework and tended to be more informally 'coffee shop' based. This avoided situations where formal, and noticeable, appointments to visit other delegations had to be arranged. As most delegation staff had multiple responsibilities then frequently the same people often came into contact in different guises which aided the building of relationships.[19] Other delegation members stressed the importance of personal relationships in enabling them to construct a picture of likely personal and state positions in specific areas.[20] The overall structure of the HLTF is a state centred inter-governmental body, that operates at the diplomatic level and draws its expertise from within the NATO context and, more especially, with firm roots in national defence and foreign affairs departments.

NATO and the Verification Community

The Verification Co-ordinating Committee (VCC)

The VCC was established by the North Atlantic Council in 1990 to co-ordinate the verification activities of NATO members, to address to planned CFE inspections.[21] The initial impetus for VCC establishment was the small number of Objects of Verification (OOV's) declared by the Soviets which made a lower than expected active inspection quota available to the Alliance. This forced the United States, which had expected to receive a much higher inspection quota, to co-operate more closely with other Alliance members to enable the maximum value to be extracted from the Alliances quota.[22] Thus it was, initially at least, national interest that forced co-operation within NATO. If the mechanism and co-ordination of the inspection process is complicated its results, in terms of detecting serious violations or discrepancies, have been unspectacular. Up to the end of the first implementation phase only minor differences between exchanged data and that recorded were reported and even those did not go before the JCG but were resolved bilaterally.[23]

Since its establishment the VCC has undertaken considerable effort to co-ordinate within the Alliance between its civilian and military elements. The HLTF and the VCC were run by diplomats whilst SHAPE had its Verification Steering Group and the Military CFE Working Group which operated under the auspices of the Integrated Military Staff.[24] The VCC meets regularly every 2-3 weeks with each member state represented by 2 individuals (one drawn from national defence ministry's the other from MFAs) and the Head of the VICS. Decisions are taken by consensus. The VCC has a more permanent personality through its Verification and Implementation Co-ordination Section (VICS) to undertake the daily tasks. Thus the VCC represents an important locus for decision-making that draws across participants spread across a wide 'diaspora' but without necessarily a great deal of stability.

Verification Implementation and Co-ordination Section

The VICS staff is relatively small - less than twenty people - comprising a mixture of directly employed staff and national secondees -mostly drawn from national verification agencies/units.[25] These individuals tend to be highly capable either in terms of IT skills, for those engaged with the VERITY computer system, or as military personnel who have worked previously as inspectors.

The VCC and VICS main tasks are of a 'co-ordinating' nature as their title suggests but also undertake a diverse range of other activities. VCC/VICS organised seminars are important activities. The first seminar was held for NATO representatives just prior to signature of the CFE Treaty. By the time a second seminar was held in January 1991, at the NATO School at Oberammergau, many previously expressed sentiments about verification being purely a national responsibility appeared to be evaporating. Subsequently efforts concentrated on harmonising internal NATO approaches to procedures, developing *aide memoires* for inspectors, escort and language training and increasingly involving the Co-operation Partners.[26] The conduct of joint inspections is managed by the VICS and it is often called upon to provide contributors to the training of national verification units. VICS staff describe their intentions as 'to make life a little easier for practitioners' by maximising the coverage that can be obtained from the deployment of resources by reducing duplication and sensibly planning commitments.

In addition to VCC co-ordination activities the Section also oversaw the establishment of VERITY, a database system that maintains the results of the combined multi-national inspection programme to which all member states and Co-operation Partners potentially have constant access. Since early 1993 the VCC, steadily began to open its resources to Eastern Co-operation Partners through NATO's Enhanced Co-operation Programme.

This began with Co-operation Partners being invited to send inspectors on some NATO led multi-national inspection visits and then offers to have their inspectors train together with those of NATO countries. This was followed from November 1993 with invitations to all Partnership members to adopt constant on-line access to VERITY.[27] The system has been subject to varying degrees of usage. Some states use VERITY to supplement their own national systems whilst others use it as the 'national' system. In some states its introduction is said to have created tensions between policy-maker and system operators with neither understanding the other resulting in mistrust and said to be responsible for fracturing in national arms control policy groupings.[28]

VICS staff say that full members are making increasing usage of VERITY especially as familiarity and training on the system increases. Terminals in member states are usually sited with the national verification units, sometimes defence ministries but only occasionally in foreign ministries (US State Department being one). This complements a picture that emerges when talking to VICS and national representation staffs in Brussels. This is the notion of a two tiered arms control community both within NATO and beyond. First, is a 'diplomatic' or 'policy-making' grouping that operates at the level of the VCC, national delegations, the defence and foreign affairs ministry's in national capitals and Vienna. The second is that of the 'operational' level represented by the VICS and by national verification agencies and defence ministry's responsible for undertaking verification activities. The VICS staff themselves appear to perceive themselves as belonging to the practitioner level suggesting that most of their work involves liaison with national verification and military units - often as a facilitator or mediator.[29]

The VICS also operates at the diplomatic level within the Alliance and there are a variety of tensions that become apparent. Several national delegation members expressed suspicion about the motives behind the actions of the VICS and fear the extension of its influence. Such bureaucratic fears are relatively normal in large competitive organisations and VICS members are themselves well aware of those concerns, believing that this acts as a brake ensuring that the Section will not be allowed to broaden its role excessively. The suspicions harboured by national delegations about the 'imperial ambitions' of the VICS continue to linger however because the length of the VCC agenda is long and continues to grow.[30] Again what we see is not a fully functioning co-operative epistemic community but tensions between competing bureaucracies and member states. There is no evidence of common causal beliefs, understandings or a common policy enterprise. The Section is often placed in the role of consensus and coalition builder in proposal formulation. In such situations where the Section is able to build a compromise it is not usually one built on expert consensus but essentially a political one. Thus it is not necessarily the knowledge base contained within the proposal that is paramount but its political 'viability'.

Within NATO two different levels of 'community' action are visible - those of 'diplomat' or 'policy-maker' and secondly 'practitioner'. The policy-maker is subject to largely national control and the primacy of national interests whilst trying to ensure that the mechanisms function to aid 'national interests'. But at the second, practitioner level, the tensions are rather different. The head of the VICS is very much a 'political' person having to operate within the parameters and guidance of the VCC - and the NATO bureaucratic environment more generally. However, below him is a staff that, though it is intimately aware of the political environment in which it operates, is trying to maximise resources by adopting an inclusive outlook that goes beyond national boundaries. Thus the VICS tends to be drawn more by its need to operate with national verification units to achieve those goals rather than through reference back to the policy-making level. The VICS staff estimated the 'arms control community' at the NATO level to number in the region of 60-80 people among NATO members plus another 50 or so from the Cooperation Partners.[31]

The Alliance as an Epistemic Community

The descriptions of the HLTF and the VCC/VICS illustrate some of the distinctions that it is possible to draw between 'policy making' and 'operational' functions on arms control within the Alliance. Some interview work at NATO HQ found that the member states were still the primary actors in managing and directing these issues. In addition to the evidence provided by the historical accounts of developments, interviewees expressed the view that ties of nationality and national organisation exert a far greater influence than any professional ties or connections through the sharing of specialist knowledge or expertise.[32] However, they also recognised that the actions of states are impacted by international organisations and in some instances domestic factors too.

The views of some of the international staff provides an interesting counterview to these points. Within the VICS the view was expressed that although it has a relatively limited role, a high degree of international cooperation takes place though if the co-operation was based more on epistemic criteria such as common understandings and beliefs rather than converging interests is much less clear This also illustrates again the distinction between the 'policy-making' and 'operational' groups. Whilst policy issues are clearly directed by states and cooperation is more sometimes more guarded at the operational level cooperation appears much more extensive based on more widely accepted common perceptions. Exploring the connections national capitals have with other groupings reveals further divergencies and complexities. Balancing varying, often competing, positions and demands undermines the case for the presence of a Haas style epistemic community based on common causal understandings and beliefs. However, at the same time there was also a recognition of the importance played by personal relationships, which in some instances were stressed as the main means by which to gain appreciations of other states or negotiators positions, and therefore ease facilitate future progress. There was considerable evidence to support the importance of informal contacts in the overall process.[33]

NATO and CFE Adaption

NATO has always been a key player in the attempts to adapt the CFE Treaty. Whilst the VCC and VICS have their focus on coordinating and implementing the existing arrangements the HLTF has been more active in the developmental process. As already mentioned it was heavily involved in the preparations for the CFE Review Conference and in particular attempts to resolve the 'Flank Problem' as its most serious deficiency. On every occasion since 1990/91 Alliance members had refused to contemplate a renegotiation of the Treaty for fear that the gains it had made would be totally lost if no new agreement could be quickly reached, preferring instead to reiterate the necessity to ensure that the current agreement was fully implemented. So NATO continued to have find solutions to a difficult mix of problems. These were the necessity to maintain the integrity of the Treaty as fully as possible, whilst actually having some sympathy for the changed environment in which the Russians found themselves in, to be balanced against the concerns of Turkey and Norway expressed about the excess numbers of TLE facing their borders.

The problem proved intractable in the continual JCG Meetings and during bi-lateral and multi-lateral discussions. Equally the solution produced at the May 1996 Review Conference in Vienna was highly unsatisfactory. Some elements were uncontroversial such as recognition of the necessity to update the Protocol on Existing Types of Conventional Armaments and Equipment (POET) which had not been reviewed since Treaty signature. Others were much more difficult. There was a compromise agreement to reduce the size of the Flank Zone and the granting of a three year transition period to allow the new limits to be met. Most controversially the facility was also granted for the Russians to 'borrow' some of the TLE quotas from Georgia and Armenia for the purpose of counting equipment. This 'temporary borrowing' of excess quotas, and the practice of 'temporary deployments' proved very unpopular and could not hope to provide a permanent resolution to the problem. So difficult had the discussions been that a significant number of statements and 'interpretive statements' were annexed to the Review Document by various of the participating states protecting their own positions and sometimes all but contradicting the main agreement.

In the wake of the 1996 Review Conference NATO and OSCE officials finally began to publicly accept, which many had already done so in private for sometime, of the necessity for a more comprehensively adapted Treaty. In an appendix to the 1996 OSCE *Lisbon Summit Document* the terms of reference for Treaty adaption were outlined.[34] The matter was also discussed during NATO-Russia Permanent Joint Council meetings.[35] Official work began on adaption in the JCG began in January 1997 though the mid to late 1998 completion timetable was over ambitious.

The main issues for the adaption process were the removal of the old

Treaty bloc structure and the zonal arrangements that had proved so problematic. Substituted for these were proposals for national and territorial ceilings and arrangements for 'temporary' and 'exceptional temporary' deployments that allowed these ceilings to be exceeded for short periods - all of which came to be incorporated in the final agreement. Clearly the issue of 'bloc limits' that had been so divisive within the North Atlantic Alliance when the original Treaty was under negotiation disappeared. In December 1998 the Brussels North Atlantic Council Meeting produced a detailed statement of CFE Adaption. As well as the commitments on ceilings and holdings of TLE, undertakings were also given that on the accession of Poland, Hungary and Czech Republic to NATO no significant Alliance forces would be permanently stationed, either directly or by the back door of 'temporary deployment' provisions, on their territory in order to help allay Russian fears about an encroaching NATO frontline.[36]

The Alliance and Arms Control Modernisation

Whilst arms control - and the CFE Treaty in particular - had been important to NATO during the late 1980s and into the 1990s with initial implementation it has slowly slipped down the NATO agenda. Obviously this is a natural reality, many of the important goals of conventional arms control were achieved, and more fundamental problems such as reformulating the functions of the Alliance, enlargement and conflicts resulting from the dissolution of Yugoslavia took on a far higher priority.

As interest in arms control - particularly that of the United States - waned and new issues advanced up the NATO agenda the pressure to maintain an active arms control agenda naturally declined too. Additionally the view also came to be expressed that the combination of CFE Treaty, Open Skies and Vienna Documents had extended the potential of 'these types of measure' to their limit and a generally pervasive fatigue with the process set in too. In many ways the implementation of the existing agreements became a 'technical' task undertaken by national verification agencies, with an element of co-ordination through the VICS with little high level political input - other than making noises over Russia and the persistent flank problem.

Given these factors then one might reasonably expect that arms control would take a back seat or its role have to adapt to changing definitions of security and the 'architecture' on the continent. Certainly it has remained in the background and its role and functions have changed little. Even the Alliances New Strategic Concept talks of continued commitments to existing measures and improving non-proliferation efforts in the areas of weapons of mass destruction.[37]

However, somewhat paradoxically, changes in the Alliances other roles are more likely to bring it into greater contact with either existing measures of arms control or in the usage of existing models in the construction new agreements to deal with specific crises. Reduction of the territorial threat to the Alliance coupled with enlargement mean that the existing measures have even less internal relevance for member states. But on the other hand, the increased role for Alliance military forces to engage in 'crisis response operations' - perhaps more likely to be 'conflict management' - may well increase the profile and relevance of confidence building and arms control measures in such locations. If Alliance military forces are to be called to intervene in either separating warring parties and/or occupying territory imposing a peace then there is a role for arms control and confidence building measures. Ensuring active participation in, and high levels of compliance with existing measures, such as information exchanges, inspection visits, activity notification etc., will at the very least, provide some advance intelligence information for Alliance forces.

Additionally, as we have seen with the Dayton Agreement (see section in chapter 4), what might be termed the 'Vienna approach' has been used as the basis for confidence building and arms control measures and further negotiations in Bosnia-Herzegovina. Though such measures in themselves cannot bring peace as part of a wider 'political' settlement they can be significant contributory factors to creating military stability. Given that such an approach has been reasonably successfully employed in the wake of the Bosnian conflict it therefore seems reasonable that we might expect to see them used again in any similar future situation where Alliance forces are involved.

Future Frameworks: NATO or OSCE?

Part of the attraction of the OSCE as the forum for the developing arms control and confidence building is in part historical and part because of its inclusivity. Historical, because the original MBFR and Vienna and CFE negotiations took place in Vienna within the margins of the CSCE process. That the process has remained centred in Vienna comes from a combination of factors. There was an inertial effect following on from the growth of the process and its linked

Table 5.1: Comparison of OSCE and EAPC Membership

State	OSCE M'ship	EAPC M'ship	State	OSCE M'ship	EAPC M'ship
Albania	✓	✓	Liechtenstien	✓	
Andorra	✓		Lithuania	✓	✓
Armenia	✓	✓	Luxembourg	✓	✓
Austria	✓	✓	Malta	✓	
Azerbaijan	✓	✓	Moldova	✓	✓
Belarus	✓	✓	Monaco	✓	
Belgium	✓	✓	Netherlands	✓	✓
Bosnia & Herz	✓		Norway	✓	✓
Bulgaria	✓	✓	Poland	✓	✓
Canada	✓	✓	Portugal	✓	✓
Croatia	✓		Romania	✓	✓
Cyprus	✓		Russia	✓	✓
Czech Rep	✓	✓	San Marino	✓	
Denmark	✓	✓	Slovak Rep	✓	✓
Estonia	✓	✓	Slovenia	✓	✓
Finland	✓	✓	Spain	✓	✓
France	✓	✓	Sweden	✓	✓
Georgia	✓	✓	Switzerland	✓	✓
Germany	✓	✓	Tajikistan	✓	✓
Greece	✓	✓	FYROM	✓	
Holy See	✓		Turkey	✓	✓
Hungary	✓	✓	Turkmen'tan	✓	✓
Iceland	✓	✓	Ukraine	✓	✓
Ireland	✓	✓	UK	✓	✓
Italy	✓	✓	USA	✓	✓
Kazakhstan	✓	✓	Uzbekistan	✓	✓
Kyrgystan	✓	✓	Yugoslavia	✓*	
Latvia	✓	✓	Totals	55	45

* membership currently suspended

coverage - importantly it also quickly incorporated the newly independent states institutional creations - JCG, OSCC and later the FSC.[38] Also the CSCE process was a very inclusive one with its 'Atlantic to the Urals' and beyond created by the collapse of the Soviet Union. Its effective membership of 54 states (with the suspension of the FRY) gives it the widest territorial membership across the continent.

The extent of C/OSCE membership was unchallenged by any other international regional organisation. But the launch of the Alliance's Partnership for Peace (PfP) programme in 1994 and its subsequent rapid growth followed by the addition of a more obvious 'political dimension' through the creation of the European Atlantic Partnership Council (EAPC) have seen the differences between the inclusivity of OSCE and PfP/EAPC membership rapidly diminish. Examination of the table below clearly illustrates the extent of duplication.

From table 5.1 it can be seen that after the accession of the Irish Republic to PfP and the EAPC the only OCSE members not part of the EAPC process are Andorra, Bosnia-Herzegovina, Croatia, Cyprus, The Holy See, Malta, Liechtenstein, Monaco, San Marino and Yugoslavia. Whilst readmission of the FRY to international institutions make take some time the EAPC includes all the states that maintain armed forces with the exception of Cyprus and some former constituent parts of the old Yugoslav Republic - and certainly all the militarily significant actors, even the traditional neutral states of Switzerland, Sweden, Finland and Austria. Therefore the coverage that the EAPC can now offer is almost indistinguishable from that of the OSCE.

The EAPC's first Action Plan agreed in December 1997 contained a significant amount of conventional arms control related activity. These included arms control orientation courses at the NATO School in Oberammergau, Joint Inspector Escort Training for CFE Cooperation Partners in the Czech Republic, further developments in the Joint Inspection programme, operation and development of the VERITY database and a number of other seminars.[39] This process effectively consolidated some of the activities of the VCC and VICS which stretched beyond NATO members for some years - especially in the field of inspector training and the VERITY database. The activities detailed in the EAPC Action Plan also extended into other fields - cooperation with OSCE, foreign & security policy planning, non-proliferation, peace-keeping, international terrorism, defence economics, democratic control of the armed forces and civil and emergency planning.[40] These are, in many cases, issues discussed within the remit of the FSC. If the security activities in and around the OSCE overlap so significantly with those of NATO - especially EAPC activities, what can justify such a duplication? Should we not transfer all of the military security activities of the OSCE to NATO in its EAPC guise. The arguments for such a transfer of functions are strong and rational. An active political element in the form of the EAPC would be a valuable complement to the more practical and vigorous PfP training, cooperation and exercise programmes.

The Case for a Transfer of Functions

The case for transferring the implementation of the CFE, Open Skies Treaties and Vienna Documents as well as the activities of the Forum for Security Cooperation can perhaps best be made on a provision by provision basis. However, first some general points can be made. The military representations on OSCE Delegations to Vienna - who tend to be individuals - are often rather isolated there. Only the United States and Russia maintain significant military presences on their OSCE delegations. This means that though there is a concentration of expertise in individuals they often have to spread their skills very thinly indeed. This often means that in some specific situations - particularly where a high technical input is required - such as with some Working Groups of the OSCC, as an example, national experts are temporarily seconded to Vienna. After their particular function is fulfilled they return to their capitals so there is no large pool of permanent expertise based in Vienna. Neither of course can the OSCE delegations operate in isolation. As well as working with their national capital foreign and defence ministries, they also have to work with their NATO and/or EU representations. Particularly in the case of NATO representations liaison was particularly important in the past with the work of the HLTF as the NATO forum for coordination prior to the main negotiations. Whilst the criticality of this contact might have diminished somewhat for those NATO members who are also EU members the growing role of the Union's CFSP and the desire to improve coordination at this level is beginning to impact on the work of the FSC in particular. Transfer of these functions to Brussels (in both its EU and NATO headquarters persona's) offers considerable scope for providing economies of scale, improving coordination and the concentration of available expertise - at least for most states. Most simply additional staff, or the better use of existing staff, on national NATO delegations in Brussels for EAPC members would reduce the requirement for further liaison and coordination and improve the utility (and probably quality) of verification expertise. When we look at the individual agreements the arguments for such a transfer of functions are compounded still further.

CFE Treaty

The meetings of the JCG could as easily be undertaken in Brussels as they are Vienna. Given the Group's function to deal with discrepancies, resolve difficulties and ensure the relevance of the Treaty it meets more frequently than originally envisaged. A concentration of expertise in Brussels would not detract from this role - indeed it could probably make problem resolution somewhat easier. Given the VCC/VICS involvement in inspector training and the conduct of joint inspections it would help ensure the congruity and relevance of the process.

Treaty on Open Skies

The implementation of the Treaty is effectively in limbo until full ratification is achieved. However, the test flights undertaken so far and the work already completed by the Sensor (and other) Working Groups should mean that when implementation comes it is likely to be relatively painless. Provisions that will allow for the accession of other OSCE states on Treaty ratification would not be affected by moving Open Skies Consultative Commission to Brussels. Again, exploiting increased concentration of expertise in one place would reduce duplication and probably the necessity to import expertise for special meetings.

Forum for Security Cooperation

The work of the FSC on implementation of the existing confidence building and norm and standard setting measures together with the ongoing security discussions undertaken in the forum could be adopted by the EAPC. Within its first year the EAPC met to discuss issues relating to Bosnia Herzegovina, the Kosovo crisis, regional security cooperation, international terrorism, WMD proliferation and defence related environmental issues among others.[41] Consultations and follow-up meetings such as those on the *Code of Conduct on Politico-Military Aspects of Security* could again as easily take place within the context of the EAPC as they are in OSCE Vienna so could the Annual Implementation Assessment Meetings required by the Vienna Documents. The concentration of expertise might even assist and speed up issues such as the problems experienced with the information exchanges that the OSCE experiences.

In technical terms too the rather more flexible VERITY based computer system is capable of supporting, probably more successfully, a continuous communication capability than has proved possible with the rather antiquated and costly 'X25' connection based OSCE system to which only 41 of the 55 OSCE participating states are connected. Efforts to improve and update the OSCE communications system to overcome its most serious deficiencies were begun more earnestly in 1998-99.[42]

The Russian 'Problem'

One of the biggest problems in undertaking a transfer of responsibility from the margins of the OSCE to NATO are Russian objections. Relations between the Alliance and Russia have always been strained since the collapse of the Soviet Union. The Russians strenuously objected to Alliance expansion with the accession negotiations of Hungary, Poland and the Czech Republic, making veiled threats in the background and refusing to countenance the further Eastwards expansion of the Alliance. The Russians also tried to negotiate a 'special relationship' with NATO that would give them a considerable influence over Alliance policy and the possibility of 'veto' in some areas. They were unsuccessful in this too though the semi-face-saving 'NATO Russia Founding Act' was signed in May 1997.[43] This was said to give the Alliance a '16 + 1' relationship. The NATO-Russia Permanent Joint Council was created by the Act that was to cover almost the entire range of cooperation issues. Part of the Act reiterated the importance of CFE adaption and the necessity for states to comply with existing arms control agreements - amongst a whole range of other issues. The relationship continues to be strained, Russia clearly unhappy with its 'second class' role, highlighted by the withdrawal of Russian participation from Alliance activities resulting from the NATO air war against Serbia over Kosovo and tensions with the creation of Alliance led KFOR. The continuing conflict in Chechnya and Alliance members criticisms of Russia ensures the tension persists.

Part of the Russian difficulties with the Alliance are linked to those with their preference in the early 1990s to see the OSCE play a more prominent security role in Europe where it felt Russia would have a more equal role. The failure of the OSCE to develop a credible Common and Comprehensive Security Model has injured Russian designs to see a strengthening in part of the OSCE's responsibilities. This will not have improved the possibility for a transfer of functions to a NATO based forum. The failure of Russia and the

Ukraine to ratify the Treaty on Open Skies so preventing its full application, linked to their difficulties with the CFE Treaty and wider internal and external differences still provides an irritating and complicating problem. Russian agreement to a transfer some of the conventional arms control functions from Vienna to Brussels, even if not formally taken over by the Alliance, could provide advantage for it. At least at the public level this would give Russia a more integral participation role in an element of Alliance policy. It would remove some of the duplication of effort that Russia, and all the other OSCE participants suffer from and would with little doubt improve the extent of internal coordination. The failure to achieve real progress in the development of the CCSM is unlikely to be overcome and reduces the utility of the OSCE as a significant contributor to security on the continent.

Conclusions

The Alliance was a natural fora for the development and coordination of its member states negotiating positions and policy. This was not always an easy process and led to significant tensions between the Americans and French in particular. Conclusion of the CFE Treaty saw the Alliance become the focus for verification coordination activities to ensure that members maximised the coverage of their inspections against the Russians in particular. But it also became the centre for multinational training activities too through the establishment of courses for inspectors. This was gradually extended to Cooperation Partners over time too. This gives the Alliance a central part in the inspection and verification process as a centre of expertise, reducing duplication and as a means of gaining limited economies of scale - the operational dimension. What the Alliance has lacked is a serious political dimension to arms control activities beyond its own membership. Meanwhile, the arms control and confidence building activities in Vienna, despite being comparatively successful, still appear to be towards the margins of OSCE activity. So far failure to develop a meaningful Common and Comprehensive Security Model and give conventional arms control and confidence building any positive sense of direction have led to a feeling of stagnation in the process. At the same time there is a continued duplication of function between some of the activities in Brussels and those in Vienna requiring an extra level of coordination.

Thus there is a firm division between, to put it crudely, 'operational' or 'practitioner' level functions located in Brussels (and states) and the 'political' level in Vienna. Bringing those functions together at NATO, would reduce duplication (the extra coordination), thus also improving consistency, bring an important policy area to the EAPC and remove the incomplete relationship that sometimes exist between these activities and the OSCE. Linking this policy area more closely with the Alliance might also ensure that the some synergy is created between the measures currently in place and the dynamism of contacts inherent in the PfP programme.

Notes

1   J. Walker, (1993), *Western Political Agendas in CFE*, Conference Paper: CFE and the future of conventional arms control, Kings College, 11-14th July, 1993, p. 1.
2   Ibid., p. 1.
3   J. Sharp, (1988), 'Conventional arms control in Europe: problems and prospects', in Stockholm International Peace Research Institute, *SIPRI Yearbook 1989: World Armaments and Disarmament*, (Oxford: Oxford University Press), p. 330.
4   J. Sharp, (1989), Stockholm International Peace Research Institute, *SIPRI Yearbook 1989: World Armaments and Disarmament*, (Oxford: Oxford University Press), p. 372.
5   Ibid., p. 380 and J. Sharp, (1988), op cit p. 330-3.
6   L. Gutjahr, (1994), *German Foreign and Defence Policy after Unification*, (Pinter: London), p. 47. See also J. Macintosh (1992), 'Confidence-building processes - CSCE and MBFR: a review and assessment', in *East-West Arms Control - Challenges for the Western Alliance*, (Routledge: London), p. 132.
7   A.C. Winner and M.J. McNerney, (1996), 'Turning Points: The Link Between Politics and Arms Control', in K.M. Kelleher, J.M.O. Sharp and L. Freedman, (eds), *The Treaty on Conventional Armed Forces in Europe: The Politics of Post-Wall Arms Control*, (Baden-Baden: Nomos Verlagsgesellschaft), p. 131.
8   J. Sharp, (1989), op. cit. p. 372.
9   R.A. Falkenrath, (1995), *Shaping Europe's Military Order: The Origins and Consequences of the CFE Treaty*, CSIA Studies in International Security, (London: MIT Press), p. 10.
10   J.M.O. Sharp, (1989), op cit p. 378.

11   D.R. Tanks, in Falkenrath, (1995), op cit, p. 15, Footnote 27. A view also supported by Jane Sharp in: K. Kelleher, J.M.O. Sharp and L. Freedman, (eds), (1996), *op. cit.* p. 86.

12   J. Rogers and P. Williams, (1994), 'The United States and CFE' in S. Croft, (ed), *The Conventional Armed Forces in Europe Treaty*, (Dartmouth: Aldershot), p. 69.

13   J. Sharp, (1988), op cit p. 331.

14   P. Gordon, (1993), *A Certain Idea of France: French Security Policy and the Gaullist Legacy*, (Princeton University Press: Princeton), p. 124.

15   Ibid., p. 15.

16   Conversation with UK FCO official, October 1996.

17   Interview with Netherlands official October 1996.

18   Interview with UK official October 1996.

19   National Delegation member, October 1996.

20   Netherlands and Canadian officials, October 1996.

21   S. Koulik and R. Kokoski, (1994), *Conventional Arms Control: Perspectives on Verification*, SIPRI, (Oxford: Oxford University Press), pp. 58-59.

22   J. Dean, (1990), 'Organisational and Institutional Issues', in *Verification of Conventional Arms Control in Europe: Technological Constraints and Opportunities*, in R. Kokoski and S. Koulik, (eds), SIPRI, (Oxford: Westview Press), p. 228.

23   Z. Lachowski, (1994), 'Conventional arms control and security co-operation in Europe', *SIPRI Yearbook 1994: World Armament and Disarmament, SIPRI*, (Oxford: Oxford University Press), pp. 566-67.

24   D. Schott and D. Aykroyd, (1992), 'NATO Training for arms Control Verification', in *Verification 1992: Peacekeeping, arms control and the environment*, J. Poole & R Guthrie (eds), (London: VERTIC), p. 152.

25   Interviews with VICS staff, October 1996.

26   D. Schott and D. Aykroyd, (1992), op cit, pp. 151-54.

27   N. Nedimoglu, (1994), 'NATO and partner countries co-operate in implementing the CFE Treaty', *NATO Review*, Vol. 42, No. 3, p. 20.

28   Conversation VICS staff, October 1996.

29   Conversation VICS staff, October 1996.

30   Discussions with national delegation members and VICS staff, October 1996.

31   Discussion with VICS staff.

32   K. Wright, (1998), *European Conventional Arms Control and Epistemic Communities*, PhD thesis, (University of Essex).

33   Ibid.

34   OSCE, *1996 Lisbon Document*, pp. 25-29.

35   C. Hain-Cole, (1997), 'Taking up the challenge of CFE Treaty adaption', *NATO Review*, Vol 45 No. 6, p. 30.

36   NATO, (1999), 'Statement on CFE', *NATO Review*, Vol 47. No 1, pp. 21-22.

37   NATO, (1999), *The Alliances Strategic Concept*, Pres Communique NAC-S(99)65, para. 40.

38   It has to be noted that of course signature to the CFE Treaty and the Treaty on Open Skies was not open to all OSCE states, but just the NATO and Warsaw Pact members.

39   NATO, (1999), *Action Plan of the Euro-Atlantic Partnership Council for 1998-2000*, Vol. 46, No 1 p. D7.

40   Ibid., D6-D9.

41   S. Balanzino, (1998), 'A Year after Sintra: achieving cooperative security through the EAPC and the PfP', *NATO Review*, Vol 46, No 3. pp. 6.

42   OSCE, (1999), *1999 Annual Implementation Assessment Meeting*, FSC.AIAM/41/99, 11th March 1999, pp. 14-15.

43   NATO, (1997), 'Founding Act on Mutual Relations , Cooperation and Security between NATO and the Russian Federation', *NATO Review*, Vol 45, No 4, p. D7.

6 Arms Control in the New Century: The Istanbul OSCE Summit

As we have seen previously, principally chapters 3 - 5, the CFE Treaty has suffered considerably from structural problems caused by the inability to adequately adapt it in the wake of the Soviet Unions collapse. Whilst the problems might have been clear actual adaption took a long time with preparatory work ongoing for sometime previously. The November 1999 OSCE Istanbul Summit was established as the agreed deadline for the signature of a new agreement which was to reflect the many changes in Europe's security environment since the original Treaty was agreed just 9 years earlier.

This chapter looks exclusively at the main changes produced by the Adapted CFE Treaty and the other measures that accompanied it in the form of the 1999 Vienna Document and the Charter for European Security. From that analysis we will see how the advances made were relatively modest and even signature of the most significant agreement - the Adapted CFE Treaty - was overshadowed by the ongoing war in Chechnya.

Adapting CFE

The adapted agreement was of necessity going to be a compromise that would satisfy the diverse interests of the participating parties. Principal amongst those would be some form of resolution to the 'Flank' problem and the establishment of 'truly' national limits to replace the old alliance ceilings on NATO and the Warsaw Pact states. In addition there was the desire to make it possible for states previously prevented from doing so to accede to the agreement. There was also a necessity to update a number of the protocols to the Treaty and permit states to vary their ceilings and holdings of TLE to provide for the vagaries of the future within specified limits.

Most of the changes to the Treaty text are relatively technical reflecting changes to the territory of the signatories, or are clarifications of the previous treaty text incorporating lessons of the verification and inspection process.

Much of the aim of the original agreement is intact but the most important changes include provisions that allow:

- States to unilaterally increase their holdings and ceilings of categories of TLE either in numerical or percentage terms but with a specified and fixed upper limit. There are also provisions for these limits to be exceeded if all of the signatories consent.
- Makes states responsible for ensuring that any forces deployed on their territory by other signatories do not exceed the specified territorial limits.
- States may also increase their territorial ceilings but to ensure overall ceilings are not raised for any state that increases its level another must consent to a reduction in its ceilings.
- Forces deployed in support of UN or OSCE resolutions are effectively excluded from the limitations of the Treaty.
- Ceilings may be temporarily exceeded if it is for the purpose of military exercises, there are forces in transit across a state or for 'temporary deployments'. Such activities have to be reported and take place within a specified time scale and can be subject to observation.
- The information exchange regime is expanded, tightened and some reports to be made quarterly rather than just annually.
- The role of the JCG is also modified to take account of other Treaty changes.
- Procedures for the accession of new signatories to the Treaty in the OSCE area are specified.

Overall these changes provide a far more flexible and therefore realistic agreement than the original Treaty which, though it was the best that could be achieved at the time, was rather static and inflexible. This flexibility should give it a less time limited character. The scope of the work of the JCG is expanded somewhat to allow that flexibility to be more institutionalised and the five yearly Review Conferences the point for integrating any changes made in the interim period.

Because of their importance for the operation of the adapted treaty the protocols detailing the national and territorial limits become the cornerstones for calculating change and are reproduced as tables 6.1 and 6.2. The declarations of individual states annexed to the agreement - and the changes already made should see a reduction to the original agreement by about 11,000 pieces of TLE.[1]

Table 6.1: Adapted CFE National Ceilings

State	MBT's	ACV's	Artillery	Aircraft	Helicopters
Armenia	220	220	285	100	50
Azerbaijan	220	220	285	100	50
Belarus (1)	1800	2600	1615	294	80
Belgium	300	989	288	209	46
Bulgaria	1475	2000	1750	235	67
Canada	77	263	32	90	13
Czech Rep. (2)	957	1367	767	230	50
Denmark	355	336	446	82	18
France	1226	3700	1192	800	374
Georgia	220	220	285	100	50
Germany	3444	3281	2255	765	280
Greece	1735	1599	1920	650	65
Hungary (3)	835	1020	840	180	108
Iceland	0	0	0	0	0
Italy	1267	1970	1818	618	142
Kazakhstan	50	200	100	15	20
Luxembourg	0	0	0	0	0
Moldova	210	210	250	50	50
Netherlands	520	864	485	230	50
Norway	170	275	491	100	24
Poland (4)	1730	2150	1610	460	130
Portugal	300	430	450	160	26
Romania	1375	2100	1475	430	120
Russia (5)	6350	11280	6315	3416	855
Slovakia (6)	478	683	383	100	40
Spain	750	1588	1276	310	80
Turkey	2795	3120	3523	750	130
Ukraine (7)	4080	5050	4040	1090	330
UK	843	3017	583	855	350
USA	1812	3037	1553	784	396

Source: OSCE

(1) Of which no more than 1,525 battle tanks, 2,175 armoured combat vehicles and 1,375 pieces of artillery in active units.

(2) Of which no more than 754 battle tanks, 1,223 armoured combat vehicles and 629 pieces of artillery in active units.

(3) Of which no more than 658 battle tanks, 1,522 armoured combat vehicles and 688 pieces of artillery in active units.

(4) Of which no more than 1,362 battle tanks, 1,924 armoured combat vehicles and 1,319 pieces of artillery in active units.

(5)   Of which no more than 5,575 battle tanks, and 5,505 pieces of artillery in
        active units.
(6)   Of which no more than 376 battle tanks, 611 armoured combat vehicles and
        314 pieces of artillery in active units.
(7)   Of which no more than 3,130 battle tanks, 4,350 armoured combat vehicles
        and 3,240 pieces of artillery in active units.

Table 6.2: Adapted CFE Territorial Ceilings

State	MBT's	ACV's	Artillery
Armenia (3,4)	220	220	285
Azerbaijan	220	220	285
Belarus (5)	1800	2600	1615
Belgium (5)	544	1505	497
Bulgaria (3,4)	1475	2000	1750
Czech Republic (5)	957	1367	767
Denmark (5)	335	336	446
France (5)	1306	3820	1292
Georgia (3,4)	220	220	285
Germany (5)	4704	6772	3407
Greece (3,4)	1735	2498	1920
Hungary (5)	835	1700	840
Iceland (3,4)	0	0	0
Italy (5)	1642	3805	2062
Kazakhstan (5)	50	200	100
Luxembourg (5)	143	174	47
Moldova (3,4)	210	210	250
Netherlands (5)	809	1220	651
Norway (3,4)	170	282	557
Poland (5)	1730	2150	1610
Portugal (5)	300	430	450
Romania (3,4)	1375	2100	1475
Russia (5)	6350	11280	6315
of which (1,3,4)	1300	2140	1680
Slovakia (5)	478	683	383
Spain (5)	891	2047	1370
Turkey (3,4)	2795	3120	3523
Ukraine (5)	4080	5050	4040
of which (2,3,4)	400	400	350
UK (5)	843	3029	583

Source: OSCE

(1)   In the Leningrad Military District, excluding the Pskov oblast; and in the
        North Caucasus Military District, excluding: the Volgograd oblast; the

Astrakhan oblast; that part of the Rostov oblast east of the line extending from Kushchevskaya to Volgodonsk to the Volgograd oblast border, including Volgodonsk; and Kushchevskaya and a narrow corridor in Krasnodar kray leading to Kushchevskaya. The territorial sub-ceiling will not be exceeded pursuant to Article VII for military exercises and temporary deployments in the category of armoured combat vehicles.

(2)   In the Odessa oblast.

(3)   States' Parties which shall increase their territorial ceilings or territorial sub-ceilings pursuant to Article V, paragraph 5, only in conjunction with a corresponding decrease, pursuant to Article V, paragraph 4, subparagraph (A), in the territorial ceilings or territorial sub-ceilings of other States' Parties.

(4)   States' Parties which shall not exceed their territorial ceilings or territorial sub-ceilings pursuant to Article VII by more than 153 battle tanks, 241 armoured combat vehicles and 140 pieces of artillery.

(5)   States' Parties which shall not exceed their territorial ceilings or territorial sub-ceilings pursuant to Article VII by more than 459 battle tanks, 723 armoured combat vehicles and 420 pieces of artillery.

Host nation consent for the deployment of military forces on their territory was strengthened in the new agreement. This measure particularly aimed at Russia saw them agree to continue negotiations on their presence in Georgia, reducing the TLE stationed there and closing the bases at Gudauta and Vaziani by July 2001. The Moldovans in an Annex to the Final Act renounced their 'right' to receive temporary deployments. Russia, having failed to reach agreement with Moldova on its continued presence there agreed to the removal or destruction of TLE there by 2001.

The new agreement is subject to national ratification and this could be its undoing. The atmosphere at the Istanbul summit in November 1999 was much less self congratulatory than had been intended. Signature of the Adapted Treaty, the 1999 Vienna Document and the launching of the European Security Charter were to be part of the meeting's highlight. Instead the continuing Russian offensive in Chechnya cast a long shadow over the summit.

The re-commencement of large scale Russian military operations in Chechnya during the Autumn of 1999 again put it in breach of the original 1990 Treaty but this time as US State Department spokesman James Rubin said

we're talking about many, many hundreds of pieces of equipment over the limits in the armour/combat vehicle category.[2]

Not only did the Russian deployment exceed the original limits but it would also exceed the new, more generous, limits of the adapted treaty too. At the Istanbul Summit Western leaders in particular put a brave face on signature of the agreement. Most said that because the Adapted Treaty could not enter into force until it was ratified by national legislatures they would not send the agreement for ratification until Russian forces had complied with the new limits. The Russians also gave an undertaking to comply with the new agreement as quickly as possible. If the new Treaty remains unratified for a long period because Russia is unable to solve its problems in Chechnya then the advances provided for in the adapted treaty could be lost entirely if it becomes 'hostage' to future events in the same way as the treaty on Open Skies has.

1999 Vienna Document

In the run up to the Istanbul Summit discussion between the participants identified a number of issues and problems that can be identified in the text that was finally agreed. The agreement on the inclusion of sub-regional measures for the first time though widespread was not met with unanimous enthusiasm. Similarly there was not significant agreement on the need to further reduce notification and observation thresholds.[3]

As is usual practice with the Vienna Documents the new agreement incorporates the measures of the previous ones. For the 1999 Document the information exchange and defence planning information arrangements are strengthened and extended and certain parts of the two rationalised to reduce duplication. Similarly the programme of military contacts and visits is re-emphasised and developed slightly with states required to submit plans of how they intend to meet these provisions. However, the threshold for the notification and observation of activities remained unaltered which was a mild surprise given the generally smaller scale of military exercises that have been conducted since the earl 1990's.

The introduction of regional measures to the CSBM regime had been frequently talked about in the past (see chapter 4) and were included in the 1999 Document. However, the measures are very guarded reflecting the caution expressed by some member states previously. It indicated that measures should:

• be in accordance with the basic OSCE principles, as enshrined in its documents;

- contribute to strengthening the security and stability of the OSCE area, including the concept of the indivisibility of security;
- add to existing transparency and confidence;
- complement, not duplicate nor replace, existing OSCE-wide CSBMs or arms control agreements;
- be in accordance with international laws and obligations;
- be consistent with the Vienna Document;
- not be detrimental to the security of third parties in the region.

Suggested measures included in the Document are: the exchange of information on defence planning, military strategy and doctrine as far as they refer to a particular regional context; further development of the provisions with regard to risk reduction; enhancement of the existing mechanism for consultation and co-operation as regards unusual military activities conducted by participating States; joint training courses and manoeuvres; intensification of military contacts and co-operation, particularly in border areas; establishment of cross-border communications networks; reduction of the thresholds for military activities, in particular with regard to border areas; reduction of the thresholds for notifications and observations of certain military activities that a State is allowed to carry out in a given period, particularly in border areas; agreement on additional inspection and evaluation visits by neighbouring States, especially in border areas; increase in the size of evaluation teams and agreement to multinational evaluation teams and the creation of bi-national or regional verification agencies to co-ordinate 'out of the region' verification activities.[4]

Charter for European Security

The Charter was the third of the agreements at the Istanbul Summit with military security implications. It attempts to strengthen some existing competences and develop new ones to make the OSCE's role in crisis situations clearer and more rapid. The main provisions cover:

- Adopting the Platform for Co-operative Security to strengthen co-operation between the OSCE and other international organisations.
- Develop the OSCE's role in peacekeeping.
- Create Rapid Expert Assistance and Co-operation Teams (REACT) to

enable quick response to requests for assistance and large civilian field operations.
- Expand the OSCE's ability to undertake police-related activities.
- Establish an Operation Centre to plan and deploy field operations.
- Strengthen the consultation within the OSCE by establishing a Preparatory Committee.[5]

The adoption of the Platform for European Security is considered by the OSCE an important element of the Charter. However, the text of the Platform reflects the difficulties mentioned in chapter 4 of finding common meaningful definitions. It still clings to the necessity to consolidate the agreements made before, ensuring their implementation and on the need for transparency, participating states and the OSCE's responsibilities to other international organisations such as the UN without providing much in the way of a sense of future direction.

The OSCE experienced great problems in establishing the Kosovo Verification Mission (KVM) during 1998-99 where it could not recruit, train and deploy adequately skilled staff sufficiently quickly. This was a significant contributory factor in its failure. The OSCE was just not experienced in preparing and undertaking operations that were to involve over 1600 personnel and require their logistical supply and communication needs. Previous field operations had generally involved only handfuls of staff. The expensive lessons of this failure appear to be addressed by the Charter, though whether they will prove adequate for future crises of course remains to be seen. The ultimate success of these measures will be highly dependent on the resources and detailed planning that participating states are prepared to invest in supporting its goals.

An Operations Centre is to be established as an element of the existing Crisis Prevention Centre. The Centre will draw upon seconded staff from the participating states and OSCE Secretariat. Its core staff will be responsible for planning and deploying field operations with the expectation that it could be expanded rapidly to deal with specific tasks.[6]

The decision to create Rapid Expert Assistance and Co-operation Teams (REACT) appears to be another lesson of the difficulties in establishing the KVM. This again looks like another earmarking process, whereby states, in conjunction with the OSCE, can identify pools of specialist expertise and other resources that could be quickly made available for deployment as part of the civilian element of any peacekeeping force - either pre or post conflict.

In its activities in Bosnia-Herzegovina, Albania and Kosovo the OSCE has had a significant input in the development of civilian policing. It has deployed personnel from participating states in support of its operations. The OSCE has also had a significant role in recruiting and training local civilian police forces and wants to develop its capabilities in this area further.

In terms of developing its peacekeeping activities the OSCE has long held a competence in this field but its only significant success in this area has been in dealing with the non-military elements - particularly in the post-conflict situation. In the Charter the Organisation reasserts its competence but appears to wish to consider an expanded role in this field though it is unclear on the direction that it may wish, or be able, to take. Clearly such an expansion of this role, particularly in the military field will be a very difficult one to manage where the interests of OSCE member states appear very divergent.

An Epistemic Effect?

In the agreement of the measures signed at Istanbul detecting the effect of any 'epistemic effect' has been very difficult. We have the common set of understandings and vocabulary which can, and was utilised which makes the technical task of agreeing text easier. What was not detectable was the presence of common goals and aims across all the delegations. In fact the opposite was probably more true. This is indicative of two things. Firstly, that even if an epistemic community or network exists in this policy area its strength is limited. It indicates the fragility of finding common goals and how dependent that is on other external factors. That in turn is a telling feature on the potential strengths and limitations of epistemic communities more widely. Secondly, it indicates just how reliant co-operation in the field of arms control is on the state of international relations rather than being a significant shaper of the international environment. Just how much this is so will be demonstrated by the ratification of the Adapted CFE Treaty. Slow or non-ratification will show that arms control as a process is of little influence on the international environment. A rapid ratification process is largely dependent on the Chechnyan crisis and Russian management of it. The key question is how heavily the meeting of international accords will weigh in the deliberations of Russian foreign policy in the area. So far the indications are not very encouraging.

Conclusions

The continuing war in Chechnya rather damaged the veneer of success at the November 1999 Istanbul Summit, traditional at such meetings. The adaption of the CFE Treaty was to be a major highlight of the event. To be sure re-negotiation had taken a considerable amount of work in agreeing new levels and the concentration of forces to be permitted. It seemed more than a little incongerous that the Adapted Treaty could be greeted with a great fanfare if it was already being breached. These difficulties highlight the continuing problems that the agreement will face. There is the need to secure an agreement that actually means something which is in competition with the desire to be as inclusive and comprehensive as possible. For the moment the greatest challenge is that posed by and for the Russians. The Russians have genuine security problems on their Southern borders. Allowing the Russians to continually operate levels of equipment in excess of those to which they have agreed will undermine the agreement. Similarly to continually criticise them for breaking its terms without being able to offer them either the means to fully comply or introduce an appropriate sanction or sanctions to bring them back into compliance also risks losing the agreement too. The almost inevitable outcome is that which has been applied during the life of the original Treaty anyway. That is tacit private recognition of the difficulties that the Russians face to be accompanied by continuing, if muted, criticism of their non-compliance with some of its actual terms. For the West the opportunities the Treaty offers to continue to observe and monitor Russian military activities is one that it will be extremely reluctant to lose entirely.

The problems are of course further complicated by the necessity for ratification of the Adapted Treaty. It is very likely that ratification will be a long drawn out process and so some sort of interim entry into force, similar to that of the original agreement, may have to be considered again. However, in today's climate such an interim step is unlikely to be easily agreed. Continuing military security problems for Russia could push ratification back indefinitely which would be likely to make it hostage to other future events and developments.

Ratification is not a problem for either the Vienna Document or the Security Charter being politically rather than legally binding as they are. For the Vienna Document the advances made beyond existing measures was rather modest. The section on regional measures reflected much of what had been discussed at the seminar on regional measures in 1997. It presents a framework menu of possible options rather than offering a more detailed list of measures for possible adaption that might suit particular types of situations. Similarly most of the other agreed measures were of an incremental nature. More significant was the failure to reduce observation thresholds. This in particular begins to indicate the more negative security environment that is slowly beginning to emerge. At the review meeting in September 1999 a number of delegations had expressed the view that thresholds should not be reduced because 'security conditions might change, requiring larger exercises'. In a similar vein the November 1999 deadline for adaption was agreed as a sensible one

> Since conditions for a successful adaption were not likely to improve after the Summit. One delegation noted that a weakened Vienna Document might result if the adaption was not completed by then.[7]

Perhaps unusually when compared to the past it was the Security Charter that produced the most concrete outcome from the Istanbul Summit. Its mixture of the more traditional OSCE platitudes such as those contained in the Security Platform on the Organisation's principles was supplemented by rather more pragmatic, and potentially much more valuable proposals. The announcements on the establishment of the Operations Centre and the REACT plan to make specialist expertise more readily available, if properly supported and financed by the participating states, it will represent an important improvement to the value and credibility of the OSCE.

Together the three measures though they have significance for dealing with the traditional military security problems that Europe faces, do little to address a burgeoning set of new security issues - both military and non-military - that are beginning to become far more urgent for much of the continent. But for the OSCE itself the difficulties remain much the same as they have been for the last few years - ensuring compliance with existing measures, finding a sense of direction, providing leadership, developing appropriate measures and coping with wider changes in the international security environment.

Notes

1   OSCE, (1999), *OSCE Newsletter*, Vol 6, No 11/12, p. 5.
2   BBC News, October 9, 1999, http://news2.thls.bbc.co.uk/hi/english/worl/ europe/newsid_4690000/469639.stm.

3   OSCE, (1999), *Review of the Implementation of all OSCE Principles and Commitments: Politico-military aspects of security*, RC(99).Jour/10, Annex 3, pp. 2-3.

4   OSCE, (1999), *Vienna Document 1999*, FSC.DOC/1/99, pp. 13-43.

5   OSCE, (1999), *Charter for European Security*, SUM.DOC/1/99, p. 1.

6   Ibid. Para 43.

7   OSCE, (1999), *Review of the Implementation of all OSCE Principles and Commitments: Politico-military aspects of security*, RC(99).Jour/10, Annex 3, pp. 2-3.

7 The New Security Environment: How Important is Arms Control in the 'New' Europe?

In the previous chapters we have looked at the recent history of conventional arms control and confidence building in Europe, the main agreements and the main international organisations which have been involved in the process to date. In this chapter we begin to look forward to the future role that conventional arms control and confidence building might have in Europe. In order to do that we have first to return to some of the fundamentals. First, what are the goals of arms control? Are they any different now when compared to the recent past? What is the place for arms control in the changed European security environment? What future measures would be the most appropriate and how could they be best achieved?

To address these issues some of the basic functions of arms control are briefly examined. This is followed by a look at some of the geographical areas from which the most serious challenges to European security might originate. To accompany this is an analysis of some of the possible 'types' of threats that the continent might face and the uncertainties that states and international organisations face in trying to predict those challenges. The chapter concludes with an attempt to predict how some of these security threats might affect the future programme for conventional arms control in Europe.

The Function of Arms Control

At the broadest level the functions of arms control can be simply put - the avoidance of war and, if that fails, the mitigation of its worst effects.[1] Clearly such goals are not solely the 'property' of those pursuing arms control, many other mechanisms and institutions have the same aims as either a primary objective or as an element of their overall purpose. These goals remain at the centre of arms control theory and policy but it is the means by which these goals are achieved that may have to be re-examined as the environment in which they are set has radically changed.

To use just one broad definition of what constitutes arms control, Jozef Goldblat has suggested that arms control is any measure that attempts to:

- freeze, limit, reduce or abolish certain categories of weapons;
- prevent certain military activities;
- regulate the deployment of armed forces;
- proscribe the transfer of some items of militarily important equipment;
- reduce the risk of accidental war;
- constrain or prohibit the use of certain weapons or methods of war;
- build confidence among states through greater openness in military matters.[2]

From such a definition we can see that the measures contained in the CFE Treaty and Vienna Documents can be viewed as arms control measures, there is no indication that there might be limits to such a process. They fit equally into the Cold War and post-Cold War situations. Therefore, if the goals remain constant what else has changed to make their continued pursuit more difficult? Can we say that these goals have already been reached by the existing measures? If they have not, are they so close to being so that further negotiations would be likely to provide only marginal improvements or not cost effective for some other reason? Or, has the European security environment so changed that we should be looking at different goals and measures to achieve them?

Where Are We Now?

The continued need for arms control and confidence building measures can be in little doubt. The end of the Cold War did not bring stability to the continent, indeed the opposite happened. Removal of the superpower straightjacket saw old conflicts remerge, and some new ones develop with considerable violence, particularly in the South and East of Europe.

The CFE Treaty and Vienna Documents as they currently exist limit some major categories of weapons, weapon system deployment, regulate force deployment and changes in those deployments and aim to prevent geographical over concentration. They contain measures that attempt to deal with 'unusual activities' and contribute to transparency by exchanging information on force levels, doctrinal change, future plans and attempt to gauge implementation of the measures through multiple and often intrusive forms of observation and verification. At the same time other measures, such as the UN register, also aim to identify the trade and transfer in conventional weapons. Whilst these agreements do not create peace and stability in themselves they do form part of a positive framework that can contribute to it.

Having made these agreements and in general seen that states are broadly complying with these commitments why is there a need to look any further? As long as the existing measures continue to be observed they go a long way to meeting the objective of preventing war in Europe but there are gaps in their coverage from both geographical and functional perspectives.

The geographic gap is small but highly important given that it applies to parts of the Balkans. Bringing in all the successor states of the former Yugoslavia to the adapted CFE Treaty would be a significant, if extremely difficult step. In terms of functional coverage we have already seen that adapting the CFE Treaty to better reflect the changed environment has proved difficult, time-consuming and is facing some difficulty in ratification. Further measures that better constrain the holdings and/or use of additional categories of weapons, logistic resources, would also be a step forward.

The issues of landmines, even with the Ottawa Convention, and light arms appear important areas that need pursuing further. Their widespread availability, ease of use, as frequently witnessed against 'soft' civilian populations in recent conflicts has pushed them higher up the agenda of conventional arms control.

The extension of NSSM's - particularly in the field of military doctrine, defence planning and democratic control of the armed forces - and ensuring that compliance was a high priority would be valuable too. As we have seen from the previous two chapters in particular, a strong political will and leadership to make such significant advances is currently absent.

And Tomorrow?

Whilst Europe lives in a changed environment with some different threats to the past, another perspective from which to approach the desirability of additional measures might be to envisage the types of threat which Europe faces and that any new measures could reduce or ameliorate. This takes us beyond the problems of the existing measures and requires identifying where the potential threats might come from and what they might actually be.

First, undertaking a geographic examination some obvious potential threat 'axes' for Europe become apparent:

- The territory of the former Soviet Union, including Russia itself. Violent conflict has already taken place in many of the successor republics and instability is still simmering in others and could escalate rapidly.
- The Balkans, more particularly former Yugoslavia, still poses serious potential problems for continued violent conflict between its constituent parts and the embroiling of neighbouring states.
- The development of serious instability and conflict in North Africa.
- Negative developments in the Middle East - especially in the areas bordering Europe.

In addition to the threat axes the 'type' of threat that each can or could pose to Europe must be considered. This introduces another set of problems which states and international organisations are currently struggling with. This includes adaption to a security environment where military security takes on a much lower priority than it did in the past and becomes just one small element of a much wider conceptual framework for security that attempts to encompass a far wider range of security threats.

The Threat Axes

Russia and the Former Soviet Union

Considerable portions of the territory of the former Soviet Union pose significant potential military security problems. Territorial conflicts have already been fought between Armenia and Azerbaijan over Nagorno-Karabakh, civil war has taken place in Georgia, Tajikistan and Dagestan, there was an uprising in Chechnya, and there is continued tension in Moldova over the Transdniestrian region. To name just some of the most prominent. The OSCE has been keen to establish a presence in all of these areas in an attempt to minimize some of the difficulties. Several of these conflicts appear in a state of stalemate which could quickly flare up again and possibly spread to other neighbouring areas too. Concern about this region is not so much about a residual Russian threat but about the instability this regional turmoil might create.

Unfortunately Russian security is perceived as not only beset by purely secessionist security problems but also seriously affected by organised crime, problems of resources scarcity (deepened by the resource intensive nature of the Russian economy), general environmental degradation, various forms of 'terrorism', potential large scale migration problems created by depopulation in some areas like Siberia, unregulated migration in Central Asia and elsewhere, plus significant influxes across the Chinese border in the Far East.[3]

The Balkans

Whilst the problems of the Balkans may have existed for hundreds of years they were largely kept in check until the beginning of the nineteen nineties. However, since then they have posed a persistent challenge for the international community which has generally responded in a less that adequate manner. The concern still remains that even after the initial wars of Yugoslav secession, war in Bosnia and Herzegovina, the Kosovo conflict with its spillover effects into Albania and Macedonia, there are still several sensitive areas remaining where conflict could explode. As such the West is already significantly engaged in long term military commitments to ensure the combatants are separated as much as possible. Further conflicts of the Kosovo 'type' could destabilize the region even further.

North Africa

Many of the military security fears relating to North African revolve around the possible activities of Islamic fundamentalists and rogue states. Since the end of the Cold War the attempt of many North African countries to maintain a form of non-aligned status has largely lost its value whilst attempts at greater integration took on an increased urgency. Related to these are the wider concerns about possible conflicts and their spillover effects that could emerge from economic disparities in the region. In some cases parlous levels of economic development and increased political fragility could combine to see collapse producing mass migration with all the attendant problems this attracts.

Potential problems also arise in the area because of the dynamics of energy supply. On the one hand Libya and Algeria are significant net exporters whilst Morocco, Mauritania and Tunisia are net energy importers.[4] The dependence on energy supplies and their cost have significant implications for economic development in particular.

It is however the fears of Islamic fundamentalists that appear to predominate in the region and for Europeans the implications that this might have for them. For virtually all of the North African states regard spreading Islamism as *the* security threat to their survival. In some of the states - particularly Morocco, Tunisia, Egypt and Algeria the situation is regarded as most serious and has become closely linked to survival of the regimes themselves. For Europe it generates concerns about an unstable, and probably hostile Southern border. The links that might be built with militant minority groups within Europe itself and economic collapse generating mass migration and further instability could become significant security issues.

The Middle East

The security threat for Europe of the Middle East has changed over the last ten years. In the past it was the possibility of deterioration in the relationship between Israel and its neighbours. But as superpower sponsorship for the two sides has waned they have been more prepared to come to the negotiating table and participate in meaningful negotiations. A serious reversal in the trend of improving relations in the Middle East could increase instability on Europe's Southern border.

Perhaps more immediately serious is the isolation of Iraq, which even with its impaired military capacity and continuation of the Northern and Southern Watch operations, could increase tension or renew hostilities again or undertake operations against its population possibly forcing migratory movements.

Threat Identification

In the post Cold War period much effort has been devoted to trying to envisage what sorts of security threats Europe will face. The emphasis has been on broadening the concept of security to cover a wider range of threats than in the past. Not just the threats posed by traditional conventional warfare and weapons of mass destruction but also trans-national crime, ethnic conflict, 'cyber-warfare', environmental degradation or disaster, to name just some of the most prominent. Work by Barry Buzan and Ole Wœver in particular have illustrated some of the considerable difficulties that these efforts face in being broad enough to be sufficiently comprehensive but not so broad as to become vague and of no value. These explore notions of economic, political and 'societal' security, some with greater success than others. But generally all of these analyses see a decrease in the prominence of 'military security' and even within that category, a reordering of military priorities too.

The difficulties of identifying new threats to security that states and international organisations face can be illustrated by reference to just two sets of institutional responses to perceived changes in the security environment. The British Government published its *Strategic Defence Review* (SDR) in July 1998. This Document established the framework against which a considerable reorganisation of British military forces was being undertaken by the newly elected Labour Government. An essential part of that review was the threat assessment to which the new force structure was to respond.[5] One section from the SDR illustrates the difficulties that Governments face very well:

- On the negative side, however, there are new risks to our security and our way of life.

- During the Cold War, the East/West confrontation dominated strategic thinking in a way that produced a misleading impression of stability in large parts of the world. In part this was because that confrontation temporarily suppressed underlying tensions and problems. In part, it was because the scale of the risks involved in the Cold War obscured the potential importance of the newer style of security risks that were emerging.

- Instability inside Europe as in Bosnia, and now Kosovo, threatens our security. Instability elsewhere - for example in Africa - may not always appear to threaten us directly. But it can do indirectly, and we cannot stand aside when it leads to massive human suffering.

- There are still very dangerous regimes in the world. Some are well armed with conventional weapons and their armouries assume greater significance as democratic countries reduce their armaments. There is an increasing danger from the proliferation of nuclear, biological and chemical technologies. As Iraq has amply demonstrated, such regimes threaten not only their neighbours but vital economic interests and even international stability.

- There are also new risks which threaten our security by attacking our way of life. Drugs and organised crime are today powerful enough to threaten the entire fabric of some societies. They certainly pose a serious threat to the well-being of our own society. We have seen new and horrifying forms of terrorism and how serious environmental degradation can cause not only immediate suffering but also dangerous instabilities. And the benefits of the information technology revolution that has swept the world are accompanied by potential new vulnerabilities.[6]

Thus we have in part an expansion for the roles of the military - humanitarian intervention and peace-keeping and operations - and a move away from territorial defence characterised by the Cold War. We also see an indication that there are new security threats in which the military may have some role too.

As the British have experienced problems in military restructuring , so too on a much larger scale, has the North Atlantic Organisation. The new *NATO Strategic Concept*, published in April 1999 provides the framework against which its military force structures and preparations are made with the important assumptions it makes over the range of threats and warning times. The section on *Security Challenges and Risks* is typically vague, illustrating the extent of uncertainty that the Alliance still feels that it faces. It would also be unfair to attribute this uncertainty solely to the fact that NATO is still trying to find a new *raison d'etre* after the demise of the Soviet threat.

The security of the Alliance remains subject to a wide variety of military and non-military risks which are multi-directional and often difficult to predict[7]

The risks are said to include:

- Uncertainty and instability around the Euro-Atlantic area and crises on its periphery. These derive from economic, social and political sources involving a combination of ethnic and religious rivalries, territorial disputes, failed attempts at reform, the abuse of human rights or the dissolution of states leading to local or regional instability.

- The existence of nuclear forces outside the Alliance which can affect security and stability.

- Area of Weapons of Mass Destruction. Fears about use of weapons but also their procurement and capabilities to produce, coupled with the increasing difficulty of detecting their technology and proliferation.[8]

• Global spread of technology making high capability and precision attack upon the Alliance assets much more possible than in the past.

• Capabilities to attack NATO information systems.

• Threats to Alliance members through other 'risks of a wider nature, including acts of terrorism, sabotage and organised crime, and by the disruption of the flow of vital resources. The uncontrolled movement of people, particularly as a consequence of armed conflicts, can also pose problems for security and stability affecting the Alliance'.

The NATO military response to these threats continues to be centred on the traditional ideas of military mobility, rapid deployment, co-operation, high levels of training, inter-operability, etc.[9]

A Threat 'Typology'?

The military responses of states such as the United Kingdom and at a larger level the North Atlantic Alliance illustrates the extent of uncertainty they consider themselves operating under. Similarly the work of researchers such as Buzan, Wœver and others form a far from comprehensive typology of threats that Europe might face in the foreseeable future. Indeed it can be argued that such a typology may well prove unhelpful, in that it could produce an over-confidence that all the alternative threats and outcomes have been identified and explored. As experience has shown it is often the unexpected combination or course of events that throws states and alliances seriously off-balance slowing decision-making and delaying their reaction. But the combination of a number of common threats that emerge from a number of these discussions and analyses, coupled with expectations of the geographical areas from which these threats might emerge, provide us with a range of possible or probable military activities and interventions from which a number of issues for arms control and confidence building can be derived.

The most significant of these threats include in some form concerns about:
• weapons of mass destruction.

- ethnic conflict.
- trans-national organised crime.
- 'cyber-warfare'.
- environmental threats.

By quickly looking at these areas individually we can identify the sorts of issues that these might raise for conventional arms control in the future.

Weapons of Mass Destruction

Of all the security threats currently being widely discussed those addressing the possible use of Nuclear Biological and Chemical (NBC) weapons are becoming the most widely feared. Whilst the concern of this book is primarily conventional arms control brief discussion of the WMD dimension is useful in providing a more complete picture.

Proliferation Issues. There are major anti-proliferation agreements for each of the nuclear, biological and chemical categories of weapons. All have been the subject of major attention since the end of the Cold War in terms of strengthening and extension. In addition to concerns about the actual growing availability of the physical technology, and frequently its dual use capability, is the growth in availability of the scientists and technologists, often from the former Soviet states, with the knowledge to develop and build weapons. A more recently documented concern is that the 'lead time' necessary to obtain basic equipment, technology and delivery means for creating WMD are shortening considerably when compared to that taken prior to the 1990s.[10]

Delivery Means. To accompany the anti-proliferation efforts have been drives such as through the Missile Technology Control Regime (MTCR), the Zangger Committee, Australia Group and the Nuclear Suppliers Group aimed at preventing the spread of the materials and their means of delivery.

Accidental Use and Accidents. The possibilities for actual accidental use of WMD have been of serious concern - especially in the former Soviet Union where fears of deteriorating hardware, or the accidental issue of false launching instructions have received widespread, if sometimes misplaced, attention. The concerns about the safety of weapons in the FSU have subsided slightly but among remaining significant concerns are those about the serious local effects that might be caused by leaks of chemicals or fissile material be they highly combustible, toxic or possibly both.

Terrorist Use. The possible use by terrorist or sub-state organisations of WMD has become a growth area of study and concern. Attacks, such as that by the Aum Shinri Kyo cult in Japan in 1995, and the 5,500 casualties it caused show the potential of even extremely crude weapons. The implications being that virtually any individual or organisation can acquire the raw materials for creating WMD with the vast problem this poses for intelligence and law enforcement agencies trying to counter them. The situations in which such weapons might be used becomes increasingly more complex and difficult to predict, detect and prevent.[11] The traditional fears about the use of WMD has gradually migrated from the use of small, dirty, nuclear weapons to the probability that it is most likely to be chemical, or some form of biological weapon that will actually be used because of the wider availability of the necessary raw materials, their means of production and delivery.[12]

The most significant factors that emerge from discussions about the use of WMD is their availability to non-state actors and the wider availability of production technology and the 'multi-use' capabilities that much of it has. This makes detection and tracking more difficult. It means that even in cases where the initial recipient has a perfectly normal, legal use for the technology there is nothing to stop a subsequent purchaser reconfiguring it to create a more sinister product.

Ethnic Conflict

Ethnic conflict very rapidly came to Europe again after the end of the Cold War. There was soon ethnic violence between Armenia and Azerbaijan and further wars have taken place in other former Soviet Republics and in Russia itself. It is however the wars in the former Yugoslavia, particularly Bosnia and Herzegovina and most recently Kosovo that have caught greatest attention in the West.

The desire to assert dominance, or conversely, independence and autonomy based upon ethnic lines in previously heterogeneously populated territory has brought vicious inter-communal violence. Large numbers of people have been physically tortured, and there has been a rapidly rising death toll as individuals, families and sometimes entire settlements have been murdered. Large numbers of others have been forcibly expelled from their homes and what they previously considered their homeland to live elsewhere, stripped of their homes, possessions and wealth. The term 'ethnic cleansing' has slipped into everyday use.

Even the military intervention of the international community through IFOR and its successor SFOR in Bosnia and the creation of KFOR in Kosovo can only stop some of the worst effects but provide little in the way of permanent resolution to the underlying problems. When such conflicts take place they generally destroy or seriously undermine the institutions and fabric of the state which makes subsequent reconstruction more difficult.

These wars show the problems that arms control and confidence building face. They cannot in themselves stop conflict where the parties do not want to be stopped. They cannot prevent the acquisition or use of heavy items of military equipment such as tanks, armoured vehicles, helicopters, artillery etc where there are others willing to supply. They cannot prevent the proliferation and use of smaller weapons such as assault weapons, anti-personnel mines, hand guns, grenades and explosives etc.

Arms control and confidence building measures cannot affect important elements of the way in which conflicts are fought, neither can they limit their immediate effects to the affected geographical area. The spillover created by conflicts can be extreme. During the Kosovo conflict not only were ethnic Albanians forced out of Kosovo into Albania and Macedonia, increasing tension still further, but there was also the distinct possibility that the pressure imposed by such mass refugee movements might have caused the Macedonian and Albanian Governments to collapse perhaps spreading the problems further afield still. The use of Alliance air power out of neighbouring states including Italian and Hungarian airfields brought fears of further extension if Serbia chose, or was able to respond in kind. Once the Serbian regime withdrew from Kosovo some refugee movements were created in the reverse direction.

Trans-national Organised Crime

Transnational crime has become another priority security issue for both states and some international organisations since the end of the Cold War. First, in attempting to halt the spread of transnational organised crime by trying to stem the movement of narcotics, extortion, illegal sales of weapons, prostitution and a host of other problems. Second, to prevent the proceeds of those activities being laundered and entering the 'open' economy. The former Soviet Union, Central and Eastern Europe, Asia and North Africa have been a focus for many of the concerns about the expansion of major international criminal activity.

In one detailed analysis of the problem Roy Godson and Phil Williams have suggested that as globalization develops the opportunities for criminal activity grow, as do the ways in which 'dirty money' can be laundered. They also assert that trans-national crime organisations typically have bases and are strongest where state authority is weak citing as examples: Italy, South America, some parts of Africa and increasingly Russia and the former Soviet Republics. There are also different organisational forms to the conduct of such activities. Some, such as the Columbian drug cartels, specialise in dealing in a single high value product. Others, such as Russian and some Asian based groups, rely on a much more diverse range of 'products' to include - drugs, extortion, counterfeiting and prostitution.

The absence of strong state authority means that criminal organisations can operate with relative impunity providing a solid base for operations to be conducted elsewhere. Conversely in some areas strong state authority, but with a lack of transparency, can provide situations which can actually foster international crime if the state views it as beneficial to itself or its members (eg exploitation by the *nomenklatura* of black marketeers as formally practised in the Soviet Union). Increasingly as organised crime gathers more financial weight and exercise greater local leverage they are beginning to 'defy, suborn or even partially supplant Government authority'.[13] Where they become very successful at this, the problem goes beyond being a law and order issue to being one of national or even international security.

One dimension of these criminal activities that has a particular relevance for conventional arms control is the trade in weapons in which organised crime often engage. If the scale of the trade becomes significant it might even extend beyond the sale of small arms and light weapons to heavier items or even treaty limited equipment. Often the most important and more immediate concern is the sale of small arms to sub-national groups that may threaten state rule, fuelling instability or even just increasing the overall level of gun violence in a society because they are widely available.

'Cyber-warfare'

This is a 'new' and rapidly evolving area of potential threat. The assumption is that the more societies become dependent on computer based technology and information then the greater the impact will be if that technology and information is disrupted. As it is true of wider society it is equally true of military use of computer based information and equipment. One definition of the threat is that cyber-warfare constitutes the *'deliberate.... and systematic attack on critical information activities which seeks to corrupt, exploit or modify information or deny service* '[14] which has both defence and non-defence based applications. The forms that the threat can take are numerous.

Data Attacks. When an opponent inserts data into an information system to disrupt it, make it malfunction or even as a source for propaganda or bogus communications to be broadcast (fake e-mails etc).

Software attacks. Similar to data attacks in that it affects data and information contained in a system. The difference being that it is not a tampering with data or stored information but the system (software) that stores and manipulates data. As such it can be made to malfunction or fail or become otherwise corrupt thus affecting more than one set of data or information and so having a much broader effect.

Hacking. The most familiar use, meaning to seize control of a system for the purpose of corrupting, stealing data, denying authorised access, secret monitoring or otherwise cause harm.

Physical attacks. Damaging the computer system itself by either destroying the building which houses it, or the system itself or the communications links to and from it using methods from lump hammer to bomb with a whole range in between.[15]

The United States has invested considerable sums in developing a military cyber-warfare capability and should be considered the most advanced military actor in the field recently vesting responsibility for the conduct of such operations in the United States Air Force's Space Command. Posing the threat we should look at a range of state actors, non-state but global actors (eg regional and religious movements), multinational corporations (against opponents in terms of intelligence and espionage) and criminal organisations to enhance their resources or to disrupt law enforcement activities against them.[16] The cost of being an actor in the IW field is falling as electronic systems become more readily available at lower and lower cost, to which can be added the important ingredients of talented individuals and sophisticated attack software which can be combined to produce a very cost effective 'strike force'.

Clearly the more dependent a military or state organisation is on computer based information then the greater the chance information disruption will have serious effects. In the context of the threat axes where generally military reliance on computer based information and systems is relatively low the less vulnerable they are to its disruption. Equally the acquisition of a capability to engage in such activities against an 'electronically dependent' enemy is likely to be beyond their means, though as already mentioned the cost of procuring such a capability appears to be falling.

Environmental Threats

Environmental security became a very fashionable concept during the 1990s and include issues of natural resource shortage and problems created by the general overuse, misuse and abuses of the planet by mankind. Specific threats can be divided into two main types - the effects of general environmental degradation and the damage caused by individual accidents or incidents. Another frequently cited dimension to the term covers possession of the necessary means to secure the supply of important raw materials - principally energy as oil or water. But as Alessandro Politi points out the 'resource scarcity' of strategic supplies has always been an issue for states.[17] Perhaps then resource scarcity should be excluded from consideration as an 'environmental' security threat.

Whilst it is not always possible to predict individual disasters or incidents the general indirect effects of environmental degradation such as - rising water levels, soil exhaustion and erosion by overcropping or poor management, the lack of water resources, etc. should be more observable at an early stage. Whilst these can be seen as serious problems in themselves, as John Vogler observes the problems are not so much of environmental damage *per se*, but more of the socio-economic problems that they create through migration, failing agriculture, increased flooding and conversely water shortage as a result.[18]

The arms control dimension of environmental security threats are more difficult to discern other than in the traditional way that environmental problems may create tensions between neighbouring states or sub-national groupings that have to be effectively managed to prevent them developing into armed conflict.

Other Threats

The sections above have dealt mainly with some of the major types of 'security threats' identified by writers and practitioners in the field that appear most pertinent to the discussions on conventional arms control here. However, other issues raised by some writers on wider security issues should not be neglected. Notions of 'political' and 'economic security' are two general headings that have received renewed attention. Sometimes the interest is in the issues for their own sakes but often because of a 'spillover' of effects that might be created by economic or political collapse. Collapsing economies could pose potential mass migration concerns as might failing political structures. They also have implications for the penetration and operations of organised crime. Others such as Buzan and Waever have paid particular attention to developing concepts of 'societal security' founded upon notions of identity based communities.[19]

Building the 'New Threats' into the Conventional Arms Control Agenda

From these analyses it is possible to factor the new security threats and the possible areas from where these threats might emerge into a synthesis of how they may affect the future conventional arms control agenda. From the brief summaries above we can draw two distinct views on possible future directions for arms control. The first, which is the most easily dismissible because of its restricted view, is that the fundamentals of arms control have really changed very little from a military perspective. The end of the Cold War and its concentration on military security might have removed the inter-bloc tension - so the source of threat might have changed - but the functions of armed forces remains to protect the state and state interests so therefore little has really altered. In effect what we are talking about is just lower levels and 'tighter' constraints for future arms control measures.

The second and much more tenable view, is that the changing emphasis in terms of the position of military security on the agenda, indeed the widening of the very concept, the process of democratic transition, but also reduced military establishments, increased levels of defence cooperation in some spheres and the conduct of international military operations on 'humanitarian' grounds, that challenge state's supremacy over their 'internal affairs' introduce a complexity beyond that previously experienced in the field of arms control.

As we have seen in the preceding chapters military security was the predominant issue in relations between the 'West' and the 'East'. Ending the Cold War inevitably challenged that dominance that the military had previously held. It became a lesser tool. As non-military conceptions gained ground armed forces and their supporting establishments shrank and were reorganised. For traditional arms control the response was relatively straightforward, just reduce the limits and lower the thresholds for notification and observation.

Widening the concept of security does not present a serious problem for arms control if the role of the military remains relatively static. However, it does become more problematic if the role of military establishments is changed to match the 'new' definitions of security threats and fulfil a role in dealing with them. Buzan *et al* make the point well when they suggest that for some states increasingly the military commitments they make are not security issues at all. The size and use of those military forces - such as peace-keeping deployments - having more to do with political and economic relations than military ones. They assert that this is especially the case for states engaged in security communities.[20]

So the challenge comes in determining how these new security issues relate to existing measures and possible new dimensions of arms control. Not all of these threats provide an obvious potential involvement for conventional military forces. For example, in dealing with weapons of mass destruction we essentially come to look at the existing non-proliferation agreements and control agreements in the biological and chemical weapons sectors rather than seeing an obvious role for conventional military forces. A similar consideration applies in the environmental sector where, apart from armed forces being a ready source of manpower to provide organised assistance in cases of natural disaster and taking on board Allesandro Polti's point that resource scarcity should not be regarded as an environmental issue, it is difficult to see a place for conventional arms control and confidence building.

When we look at the final three issues of the threat areas addressed - ethnic conflict, trans-national organised crime and 'cyber-warfare' the picture becomes rather more interesting and complex.

'Cyber-warfare'

This issue is perhaps the more straightforward to directly address. It is still a capability that is in its infancy and where few states appear yet to have invested heavily in developing quality defensive and offensive capabilities apart from the United States. It is no doubt an area where capabilities will continue to evolve rapidly. Some of the vulnerabilities have been discussed previously but the levels of response are almost as varied as the potential threat. The lowest levels can include very simple efforts to improve security by physical measures of system protection, reducing possibilities for unauthorised access, making buildings secure through to security programmes that attempt to detect and halt unauthorised access to systems. Offensive capabilities include the use of one's own equipment and personnel to inflict significant damage on an opponents civil and military computer based infrastructure and warfare capabilities. The area is also complicated because of the increasing ability of non-state actors to acquire IW capabilities as the equipment becomes financially cheaper, minaturised and easy to conceal. But to bring it into the realm of arms control requires some fairly widespread agreement on the necessity to restrict it. Even in the unlikely circumstances that this could be done, serious control would be difficult. But confidence building - such as the demonstrations and presentations required for the introduction of new weapons systems - ought to be possible.

A more difficult aspect to deal with are those aspects of information warfare that might affect non-military governmental and commercial sectors. It is probably more appropriate that such threats, especially where they originate from a non-military source, be dealt with by police, intelligence and specialised agencies.

Trans-national Organised Crime

Some of the difficulties that are posed to a state by transnational organised crime have been outlined above. There it was mentioned that crime appears to flourish most when state structure is weak. Where this is the case the question becomes not so much determining how the military might be involved in countering trans-national crime but asking the question of should it be involved at all? If it should, what are the limits on the extent of participation and the tasks it should fulfil? Whilst most would accept the military, as a legitimate arm of the state, should provide some support to the 'civil authority', particularly in times of crisis, the problem is essentially then an internal security one.

Ethnic Conflict

The issues posed to arms control by ethnic conflict are those where we have most experience in comparison to the other two. It also appears to be the most serious in terms of its potential for loss of life. Where a state turns upon part of itself there is not only immense damage, loss of life and long term division created in the area, but there is also the fear of contagion across surrounding borders and areas. Thus there are problems for arms control and confidence, like who has what weapons and what is their legal title to them. Is their deployment worrying their neighbours sufficiently to trigger provisions like those on Unusual and Hazardous Military Incidents, contained in the Vienna Documents?

A complimentary problem that we have witnessed when the international community acts is how operations such as those of IFOR/SFOR and KFOR have required deployments from participants that infringe existing CFE Treaty and Vienna Document's provisions.[21]

Military, Paramilitary, Police Forces and Internal Security

The continued references to the problems these threats pose for internal security is essentially a sharper continuation of a problem that often arose in the CFE and Vienna Document discussions over the inclusion of security forces personnel and equipment in the negotiations. In many states internal security forces hold items of equipment - such as armoured infantry fighting vehicles and helicopters - that if they were in the hands of 'military' formations would be classed as TLE in the context of CFE provisions. It has to be recalled that in some European states the separation between police and military forces is difficult to make and even where it has been made the roots of that separation are often not very deep. This can blur the distinction between internal and external security still further.

The development of menus of measures such as with the 1993 agreement for 'crisis stabilizing measures' which could be invoked in the case of internal, sub-national or ethnic conflict face severe problems. In the case of the civil war as they would need application at the sub-national level, those involved in such a conflict are unlikely to feel fully bound by the provisions of international norms and agreements, or appeal to them, unless they feel it temporarily benefits them. Conflict in the former Yugoslavia must stand as the obvious example of this.

Conclusions

From the discussions in this chapter a number of threads can be brought together. From Goldblat's adopted definition of arms control it is clear that its goals still have an intuitive importance for us today. The provisions in measures such as the Vienna Documents, the CFE Treaty and the Treaty on Open Skies have an important part to play in managing the continents military relations though they are far from perfect and further refinement should continue. Thus we have the continuation and rationalisation and extension of existing qualitative and quantitative measures to consider. Additional tools such as the UN Register on conventional arms transfers aid the process too.

When we look at geographically adjacent areas to Western Europe, the territory of the former Soviet Union, the Balkans and possibly North Africa and the Middle East are likely to pose real or potential threats to European security for sometime to come. Look further afield and you can draw scenarios for threats to Europe that might come from the Far East and other areas of the world. When we look at the types of threat that might be posed from some or all of those areas we can see something somewhat different from the past. The fear of outright territorial conflict appears to be at a lower level than probably at any other time in the last hundred years or so - at least in Western Europe.

Meanwhile there are still serious concerns about the possible use of weapons of mass destruction, even on a limited or terrorist scale. Whilst ethnic based war has already been witnessed in the fallout from Yugoslav secession and in some former Soviet Republics, and there is the distinct possibility that yet more might still occur, trans-national organised crime, environmental threats and 'cyber-warfare' to name just some have been identified as possible serious threats for the immediate future. In all of these categories the role that conventional arms control can play is likely to be strictly limited. Where it does have a part to play they quickly begin to impinge on traditional notions of internal security, until now considered as sacrosanct preserves of the 'nation-state'. Thus we appear to be faced with a dilemma. In the first instance the existing gains need to be consolidated and perhaps improved still further. In the second, serious consideration needs to be given over the preparedness to engage on further measures, perhaps in forms that significantly depart from the constraints of the past, that deeply penetrate a state's internal security concerns and deflate the idea of national sovereignty still further.

The experience so far suggests that it is only the first alternative that is likely to secure anything like widespread support among the members of the

OSCE, NATO and EU. This reflects as much upon an adherence to the practices and experiences of the past as any readjustment to the changed security environment about which most states and international organisations talk about. It is also likely that it will be qualitative measures that will be of more significance than quantitative ones. If this is true then it may well be that to ensure their effectiveness the verification of new qualitative measures will have to be of a better quality than those that we already have. But the big question is can the states of Europe be persuaded to adopt further measures that go beyond the existing style of arms control and confidence building and what expectations and problems might this pose amongst state and international organisations involved?

Notes

1   H. Beach, (1995), 'Arms Control in Europe after the Cold War', in C. Bluth, E. Kirchner and J. Sperling (eds), *The Future of European Security*, (Aldershot: Dartmouth), p. 137.

2   J. Goldblat, (1994), 'Basic Concepts' in *Arms Control: A Guide to Negotiations and Agreements*, (London: Sage), p. 3.

3   S. Medvedev, (1998), 'Former Soviet Union', in P.B. Stares, (ed), *the New Security Agenda: A Global Survey*, (Washington DC: Brookings Institution Press).

4   F. Faria and A. Vasconcelos, (1996), *Security in Northern Africa: Ambiguity and Reality*, Chaillot Paper No. 25, (Paris: WEU Institute for Strategic Studies), pp. 3-4.

5   HMSO, (July 1998), *Strategic Defence Review*, HMSO, (electronically available from http://www.mod.uk).

6   Ministry of Defence, (1998), *Strategic Defence Review*, (Chapter 1).

7   NATO, (1999), *The Alliance's Strategic Concept*, Press Communique NAC-S(99)65, paras 20-25.

8   Clearly the Alliance is beginning to attach considerable importance to this threat area with the announcement of its WMD Initiative after the Brussels Summit this year. *Washington Summit Communique*, Press Release NAC-S(99)64 para 30-31.

9   NATO, (1999), *The Alliance's Strategic Concept*, Press Communique NAC-S(99)65.

10   W. Schneider, (June 1999), *Findings of the Rumsfield Commission: Threats from the Proliferation of Ballistic Missiles and Weapons of Mass Destruction - and Possible Remedies*, (Conference, Middlesex University, UK, June 1999).

11   S.R. Bowers and K.R. Keys, (1998), *Technology and Terrorism: the New Threat for the Millennium*, (London: Research Institute for the Study of Conflict), pp. 19-22.

12   A. Politi, (1997), 'Western Europe', in P.B. Stares, op. cit. pp. 39-40.

13   Ibid. p. 67.

14   A. Rathmell, (1997), 'Cyber Terrorism: the Shape of Future Conflict', *RUSI Journal*, Oct 1997, pp. 40-46.

15   CSIS, (1998), *Cyber crime, Cyber terrorism, Cyber warfare: averting an electronic Waterloo*, (CSIS Press: Washington DC), pp. 10-11.

16   Ibid. p. 26-7.

17   A. Politi, (1998), op. cit. p. 125.

18   J. Vogler, (1997), 'Environment and Natural Resources', in *Issues in World Politics*, B. White, R. Little and M. Smith, (eds), (Basingstoke: Macmillan), p. 233.

19   B. Buzan, O. Waever, and J. de Wilde, (1998), *Security: a New Framework for Analysis*, (London Lynne Reinner), O. Wœver, B. Buzan, M. Kelstrup and P. Lemaitre, (1993), *Identity, Migration and the New Security Agenda in Europe*, (London: Pinter Publishers).

20   B. Buzan et al, (1998), op. cit. p. 49.

21   Addressed in the Adapted CFE Treaty.

8   The Future: Small Steps

As we have seen in the preceding chapters there are many real and potential challenges to the successful continued operation of the arms control and confidence building arrangements currently applicable to most of Europe. It is also true in the context of the changing European security environment in terms of both the institutional structure that could evolve and the problems with which any security 'architecture' will have to deal.

We have also looked at the fundamentals of epistemic community and network theory and how such a community might have been considered to have existed in this field, based principally around Vienna from the mid nineteen-eighties into the early nineteen-nineties. It has also been possible to witness how, even if such a community did exist at some time, the less positive security environment of the later nineteen nineties saw cooperation in the field slow as state interests began to assert themselves more strongly again. Thus the purpose of this chapter is to draw some conclusions on both elements of this study.

Conventional Arms Control as an Epistemic Community

Certainly Vienna in the mid-nineteen eighties was likely to be a fertile environment for the development of an epistemic community in the field of conventional arms control as the two blocs began to enter into more meaningful negotiations than had previously been possible.

But as was also seen the relatively high turnover of staff in the field appears to be indicative in most cases that few, if any, individual's expertise is regarded as of such particular importance so as to require them to remain in Vienna for periods significantly longer than most of their contemporaries. This enables the significance of individuals within the arms control process to be questioned, showing a greater importance on the process rather than the role of any individual, and brings closer to the fore the importance of institutional (national) affiliations rather than personal attributes. Given the significance attributed by Rhodes and Marsh and, Martin Smith about the importance in continuity of a limited number of actors, (though not necessarily individuals) this would suggest that, in their terms, conventional arms control is in fact a 'policy network' rather than a 'policy community'. The placing of individuals into diplomatic posts provides a well defined framework against which state participants undertake their own work providing formalised, ready contact and access points and the framework for liaison between them. This enables the range of activities in which participants are involved to be defined, the range of possible national positions and policy options (policy enterprise) to be identified and the provision of a common vocabulary to emerge as discussion moves in an increasingly technical direction from the initial, well understood form of diplomatic terms and associated meanings. In short it is a developing base for the socialisation of participants. These factors present a framework against which it may be possible to establish the existence of an epistemic community. However, the role of individuals should not be totally overlooked. As Winner and McNerney observe the replacement of Stephen Ledogar, a diplomat, with James Woolsey, an arms control expert, as Head of the US Delegation in autumn 1989 was a signal to the Soviets that the Americans were prepared to speed up negotiations.[1]

What has not been clearly visible are forms of evidence that would indicate that at any time there has been the presence of a strong community in Vienna that significantly cuts across national and alliance boundaries. There is no strong evidence of a core group of individuals, based in Vienna, in the long term who have participated in arms control for a prolonged period. Indeed it is other considerations that have been of greater significance in determining delegation sizes over the years.

It is also true to say that since the height of events roughly between 1989-92 there has been a decline in the interest shown in discussions in Vienna for a number of reasons as conventional arms control has slipped down the international security agenda. With such a decline in intensity and interest there has generally been a commensurate decline within the participating states to ensure that a continuity of personnel remain at the heart of the process to ensure individuals state's interest are most successfully served.

Conventional Arms Control and the Haas Criteria

The Haas model of epistemic communities offered some advantages to other 'network' and 'policy community' approaches. It positively defined standards of what constitutes an epistemic community. But operationalising the criteria and the research agenda is extremely difficult. Adequate access to information to pursue Haas's research agenda is problematic. Even where information is available, much of the data can be sufficiently ambiguous to allow a variety of interpretations to be made. Instances of this include determining individuals belief and values from any written output they produce, establishing the significance of particular institutional affiliations, the establishment of sufficiently narrow definitions of key values and causal beliefs below a generalised level for a given policy area. Thus in the strict terms of the Haas criteria there is no overwhelming evidence to suggest the presence of a strong epistemic community in arms control. However, whilst the Haas model may have some serious flaws, to reject it entirely would be foolish as it contains some important and useful elements of relevance in examining policy processes.

Knowledge has a part to play but it is clearly impacted by the more traditional interplay of 'power' concerns.

In addition to some of the methodological problems outlined above, there are other difficulties that can be aggregated to a more general level too. Foremost among these is the role of high level leadership - mainly at foreign minister level, which in this field at least, is closely connected to the 'national interest' even where this is   poorly defined. Questions of interest are also connected to notions of certainty. The relative, and changing, strength of these factors impacts upon the role and strength of the arms control 'community'.

Leadership

During the 1980s, leadership in arms control was generally very obvious. A state either looked to the Soviet Union or the United States. If a NATO member, policies tended to follow to a greater extent those of the US, or the 'Quint' and smaller member states generally had little option but to follow. In the Eastern bloc the Soviets provided leadership, generally to the exclusion of other state parties. As Soviet leadership declined the NSWTO states, especially Hungary and Poland, began, with growing confidence, to assert their emergent national interests.

Both superpowers were criticised for the coercion they exercised. Since the major agreements and the fracturing of the Soviet Union, leadership has been much less in evidence. As the chapters on current activities in Vienna demonstrate some bemoan the absence of strong leadership to provide an ongoing dynamic to push the process forward and want some form of leadership to emerge. Yet, when the old leaderships occasionally reassert themselves there are again complaints from the NATO camp about the 'hegemonic nature' of American leadership and the way Russian interests are put ahead of other Soviet successor states. This happened most noticeably at the March 1996 CFE Review Conference when European states were unable to reach agreement, but US and Russian negotiators compromised on the flank issue over the heads of other participants.[2]

If a strong transnational community existed in arms control it could be expected that the community would be a useful method by which to generate leadership in the field through agenda formation. This has clearly been lacking in Vienna. The absence of a well defined agenda, and the reactive nature of activities in the field - such as the Dayton arms control provisions, helps to reflect the lack of leadership. This is related to national interest definition. In

Brussels although the focus is more closely linked to implementation, the existence of the VCC/VICS is seen as a significant influence on agenda formation even if in a restricted field.

National Interest

The extent of national interest definition has fluctuated considerably, both over time and between states in the last 10 years. For many years the lack of serious negotiations meant that although the term 'national interest' was often expressed, detailed conceptions of what those national interests actually comprised were often poorly defined. The bloc environment also made those interests easier to define because the boundaries of bloc allegiance were much clearer and superpower leadership often compensated for, or overwhelmed, the need for national decision-making mechanisms.

Additionally national interests were aggregated at different levels. For example there were frequent public expressions at foreign minister level of state delegations that it was in their state's 'national interests' to reach an agreement. At the actual negotiations these were more flexibly interpreted. As events and negotiations unfolded the detail of policy was filled in as diplomats and experts were able to provide information on those events and negotiations and the positions of other actors, as Radaelli terms it 'interest becomes a dynamic 'dependent' variable, framed by knowledge'.[3] Where positions were well established then flexibility on the part of the diplomats and experts was generally lower than where there was no clear direction or instructions leaving greater room for manoeuvre and technical expertise to operate. This expertise had to operate within the mandates, instructions or limitations presented by national governments.

The fact that there is so little sense of direction to the Vienna process for the last few years speaks for the absence of an arms control community. If a strong community existed that was based on principles it would have provided some overall leadership, and through that direction impart knowledge and information to inform national interests that would probably be more uniform across the participants. No such influence is clearly visible. What is more the case is that knowledge has a strong role but its possession and application are quickly overridden when national interests, however defined - and this can include a role for experts in defining those interests - dictates. The linkage exists because for transnational expert communities of any significant size to exist contact is most likely to take part through institutional forms -

most likely international organisations.

Peter Haas suggests the need to define interests is one significant reason why governments resort to using epistemic communities. Whilst a fully fledged epistemic community of the Haas type can help define interests, it would of course not be the only body willing or able to fulfil this function. 'Lesser' policy communities and networks can be equally useful but such a weaker grouping is thought less likely to be as persuasive in making its position and views felt. The substantial difficulties some states seem to have in defining their interests in the field of arms control support the view that it is not an epistemic community in operation but probably some different form of policy formulation. Perhaps then the value of the epistemic community, or similar models, might not be for use as independent variables but more as 'intervening' ones, which can impact upon the policy process.

Other Network and Community Approaches to Policy-making

Clearly interest in network, policy networks and policy communities will continue, but there seem to be almost as many variations of these models as there are researchers undertaking the work. The problem with many of the competing definitions that have been provided so far is that they are insufficiently detailed. The work of Rod Rhodes in particular has been useful in outlining the range of networks and communities and placing them on a continuum. But when it comes to detailed examination, Peter Haas's definition, with all its faults, is still ahead of others in that it has attempted to 'pencil in' some detail to the outline concept. Most researchers have so far used only very broad comparative techniques, but in only comparing 'outlines' important supporting or contradictory evidence of case studies is lost. Increased detail is likely to flag up more clearly distinct differences that would make classification more precise. Without proper detail, Claudio Radaelli's concerns about the problems of drawing macro-micro level linkages are well justified.[4]

Thus it is important that not all small or closed policy communities are simply given 'epistemic status' until they are really shown to be so which has recently been the tendency.[5] Without such demonstrations Peter Haas's model is devalued and important data on different forms or characteristics on other 'types' of policy community might well be lost or overlooked. Thus whilst it would be easy to describe the conventional arms control 'community', at the broadest level of abstraction, as an epistemic community, the more detailed evaluation clearly shows it not to be so. Therefore the challenge is to undertake both comparative and specific research in related and unrelated policy areas of sufficient detail to allow close comparisons to be drawn and a more rigorously defined model to be developed.

Future Developments in Arms Control

As we have seen since the frenetic activity in arms control peaked by 1992 its pace has been far more pedestrian. Explaining the causes and consequences of this touches upon a large number of factors. All through the 1970s the possibility that the levels of military equipment compressed into Europe could be reduced was always just out of reach. When change came it was very rapid and it was not therefore unrealistic to expect a period of consolidation afterwards. This pause was necessary as the clutch of agreements imposed a significant burden on a large number of states to reduce and destroy or dispose of large amounts of military equipment and required the establishment of mechanisms and institutions to oversee this process. It was also complemented by similar activities in the creation and operation of verification units and supporting bodies and all of which took time to implement and mature. The slow and expensive process of equipment destruction required by CFE in some states meant that the original deadlines were not fully met.

But the political environment for which these agreements were primarily designed has been shattered and what is to replace it is still far from clear. Therefore as the study has shown the direction imparted by the old political environment has disappeared and together with it firm ideas about the form future measures should take. First, has arms control reached its limit? In technical terms it has not, but the will to pursue such measures much further has certainly evaporated. Proposals resurface periodically - such as on the desirability to include naval activities - to broaden the arms control agenda further but often receive only lukewarm interest.[6] There have also been measures that have emerged in recent Vienna Documents designed to improve the coherence of the provisions in some of the previous agreements.

It is somewhat ironic that there appears to be more than a grain of truth in the belief that devising arms control measures is most easy when they are not necessary, or phrased another way that progress in arms control is more a reflection of international relations than an influence upon it.[7] Thus this could be an explanation for developments up to the mid 1990s, as the improvement in relations between the US and Soviet Union took place. It also provides an explanation for the current situation where events particularly in Bosnia, Kosovo, Chechnya stir old suspicions and create further uncertainties. If the uncertainty lifts will the path of future developments become clearer? Indeed it is in conditions of uncertainty that epistemic communities are said to come into their own. If divisions - particularly those involving Russia - were to continue to deepen further then additional measures might become more necessary but difficult to achieve. If the relationships were to be rebuilt then the measures would be less necessary but progress might be easier.

The question of continued US interest in European conventional arms control ought to be raised too. Much of the United States interest in Europe was attributed to origins with George Kennan and the implementation of containment theory. If restraining Russia is no longer to be considered of key importance where would US interest in Europe go? First, it has to be recognised that the US is 'locked into' the existing agreements and measures for as long as they exist in their current form. But the extent of their active participation could, and already has, significantly declined. As mentioned at various points in the study many Western diplomats already bemoan the reduced leadership role played by the US in providing a dynamic to the negotiation process - even though aimed at looking after US interests. Even a reduced level of US interest is survivable provided there are no major challenges to the system. However, if different configurations of state alignments begin to develop then the existing arrangements could be severely unsettled. Increasing general cohesion among the EU states as it more actively pursues development of a Common Foreign and Security Policy might well antagonise the US - or Russia - if they feel their position in the process is threatened and provides another linkage point for disputes in other policy areas. Such antagonisms could threaten progress and the current institutional structure and because of the significant dependence on unanimity within the OSCE make it possible for single states to block further arms control developments.

Having frequently talked about 'progress' what form could further measures take. There is undoubtedly fatigue in developing existing forms of measures still further. Evidence for this rests largely in the fact that measures in the 1994 and 1995 Vienna Documents are of a consolidatory nature rather than a progressive one and further measures in the 1999 Vienna Document modest to say the least. Development of the Common Comprehensive Security Model has proved extremely difficult for a host of reasons too. But as Kenneth Adelman has observed in relation to strategic weapons at lower levels of equipment holdings, cheating on agreed limits takes on greater significance. Exceeding say the MBT quota by 100 when the agreed holding is 2,500 doesn't mean much but when this is reduced to 500 the excess can be of importance.[8] The existing measures, supported by the verification regime, appear adequate for limiting the specified categories of military equipment, ensuring exchanges of information on stationing, staffing, equipment and future plans. But to go further requires considerable innovation and might well change the entire rationale for their existence. The extension of measures to further areas or categories of forces or equipment is possible, as would be the tightening of existing provisions say on sizes of notifiable exercises etc. but again these are incremental rather than 'radical' steps. Extension of measures to monitoring production could be more innovative but are partially met by the provisions of the UN Conventional Arms Control Register. The greatest challenge at the moment remains ratifying and implementing the Adapted CFE Treaty and the continued harmonisation of existing measures and their extension to a wider range of participants. Harmonisation that ensures the uniform application of the Vienna Document, CFE, and Treaty on Open Skies provisions would eliminate a number of anomalies in participation and ensure maximum engagement in the process.

Developing measures that would constrain the equipment or activities of internal security - or even para-military - forces are more potentially rewarding. Such measures could be pragmatically justified on the basis that considerable amounts of TLE -such as ACV's/AIFV's and helicopters have been transferred to internal security forces in former Soviet republics and therefore outside existing provisions, which could be returned to the military at any time. In terms of arguments over state sovereignty, few states would be prepared to abrogate their jealously guarded 'right' to manage their internal security and undermine such a principle of international law. But events most recently as those of NATO's air campaign in Kosovo during 1999 challenge those perceptions whatever the technical legality of the intervention. Similar to the arguments over arms control those states most likely to 'need' regulation are likely to be those most reluctant to agree to it, making progress next to impossible. If it becomes possible then it is most likely not to be very necessary!

The development of comprehensive 'crisis stabilizing measures' or other measures which could be invoked in the case of internal, sub-national or ethnic conflict would also be a great step forward. The existing provisions on this subject agreed in 1993 are extremely modest, being adaptions of existing

CSBM provisions and are difficult to implement.[9] The problems with such measures is that because they may need application at the sub-national level, those involved in sub-national conflict are unlikely to feel fully bound by the provisions of international norms and agreements, unless they feel it temporarily benefits them. Conflict in the former Yugoslavia must stand as the obvious example of this. Implementation of the arms control and confidence-building measures in the Dayton Accords was only possible when peace was imposed on the combatants with the threat of coercive force and economic devastation if they did not cooperate.

Given the possible problems highlighted in trying to develop further measures perhaps a more basic question needs investigation. That is: are further conventional arms control measures and associated verification provisions needed at all? In the short-term, probably not in any substantial sense. As Antonia and Abraham Chayes argued, it is dispute settlement mechanisms that are worthy of more attention than further control and constraining measures and verification.[10] But to achieve this is a longer term goal to which efforts should be directed even though it will require over-coming considerable inertia. Development of further measures that constrain or reduce weapon holding levels, expand the numbers of affected categories, improve the content and time period of the information exchange regime, if they can be agreed at a time when not highly necessary they can become an important hedge against future revisionism or back-sliding. The 'tying in' of participants to an increasingly more complex and expansive regime is one means to prevent disengagement from it. This is especially true when the context of other institutional security connections in the form of NATO, WEU/EU, OSCE and bilateral arrangements are superimposed on that of arms control too. But to make this successful states have to continue to be convinced that these institutions affect their 'vital interests' to ensure they do not let them fall into disuse or become subject to open abuse without punishment.

We are perhaps already beginning to see a stage in the evolution of the approach to future measures. As already mentioned there have been expressions of fatigue in developing further CSBM and arms control measures in the mould of the existing measures. The OSCE's 'Framework for Arms Control' together with the document on 'Development of the Agenda of the FSC' appear mostly ambitious 'wish lists'. Within them are pledges to introduce more Norm and Standard Setting Measures (NSSMs) of the type already reached on the Code of Conduct on Politico - Military Aspects of Security, the Guidelines Governing Conventional Arms Transfers and Principles Governing Non-

Proliferation.[11] Whilst this may represent a stage in the evolution of developing future measures, the problem with them is that because they are so generalised they are regarded as being 'weak measures', difficult to confirm or verify. The use of 'norms' as a frame of reference for these agreements, rather than quantifiable or measurable elements, makes adequate verification very difficult but that should not stop us from trying to develop them. Success could be very rewarding to ensure that the effects of violent conflict, if it has to happen, is minimised as much as possible.

Notes

1   A.C. Winner and M.J. McNerney, (1996), 'Turning Points: The Link Between Politics and Arms Control', in K.M. Kelleher, J.M.O. Sharp and L. Freedman, (eds), *The Treaty on Conventional Armed Forces in Europe: The Politics of Post-Wall Arms Control*, (Baden-Baden: Nomos Verlagsgesellschaft), p. 145.

2   Discussions with UK officials, March 1997.

3   C.M. Radaelli, (1995), 'The role of knowledge in the policy process', *Journal of European Public Policy*, Vol. 2., No. 2, p. 165.

4   Ibid. pp. 172-3.

5   See G. Dudley and J. Richardson, (1996), 'Why does policy change over time? Adversarial policy communities, alternative policy arenas, and British trunk roads policy 1945-95', *Journal of European Public Policy*, Vol. 3, No. 1, p. 69, as an example of this common practise.

6   Annex to FSC.DEC/9/96

7   J.M.O. Sharp, (1991), 'Conventional Arms Control in Europe', *SIPRI Yearbook 1991: World Armaments and Disarmaments*, (Oxford: Oxford University Press), p. 457.

8   K.L Adelman, (1990), 'Why Verification is More Difficult (and Less Important)', *International Security*, Vol 14, No. 4, p. 145.

9   FSC Journal No. 49, Annex 2.

10   A.H. Chayes and A. Chayes, (1990), 'From Law Enforcement to Dispute Settlement: A New Approach to Arms Control Verification and Compliance', *International Security*, Vol. 14, No. 4, pp. 154-55.

11   Section IV, FSC.DEC 9/96.

Index

SEVEN DAY LOAN
This book is to be returned on
or before the date stamped below

2 1 OCT 2002

1 1 DEC 2002

1 4 JAN 2003

3 0 SEP 2003

1 7 OCT 2003

- 7 NOV 2003

1 7 NOV 2003

1 6 DEC 2003

1 3 JAN 2004

1 5 JAN 2009